FLORIDA STATE UNIVERSITY INSTITUTE ON WORLD WAR II

THE HUMAN EXPERIENCE

with the Oliver L. Austin, Jr., Slide Collection & the World War II Writers' Weekend
G. Kurt Piehler, Curator

BILL MAULDIN
AN ARTIST ON THE FRONT
&
THE DESIGN OF WAR
WORLD WAR II PROPAGANDA POSTERS & FLAGS

from the Collection of Patrick M. Rowe

WITNESS TO WAR

Selected photographs organized by The John and Mable Ringling Museum of Art
from the Collection of the Institute on World War II and the Ringling's Coville Collection

February 13 - March 29, 2015
Florida State University
Museum of Fine Arts

This Program is Sponsored in Part by: The Florida State University Art & Humanities Program Enhancement Grant; The City of Tallahassee State Partners Initiative and the Leon County Cultural Development Program, both administered by the Council on Culture and Art; The 2015 Peace on Earth Gift; and with the support of the 2015 Opening Nights Festival.

FLORIDA STATE UNIVERSITY INSTITUTE ON WORLD WAR II

The exhibition of art and artifacts on World War II was organized by the Florida State University Museum of Fine Arts in concert with Guest Curator Dr. G. Kurt Piehler and the staff at the Institute on World War II and the Human Experience, among them Anne Marsh, Registrar for the Collection. Loans of art and artifacts from Dr. Patrick M. Rowe were made possible through his research and generosity. MoFA Project Staff: Allys Palladino-Craig, Editor and Grant Writer; Jean D. Young, Registrar and Book Designer; Teri R. Abstein, Curator of Education; Jasmine VanWeelden, Communications; Wayne T. Vonada, Jr., Preparator / Installation Designer; Rosalina Zindler, Fiscal Officer; Art History Graduate Assistant (Editorial and Registrarial) for the Project: Colleen Bowen.

In Memoriam
William Oldson (1940-2014)
Professor of History, Florida State University
Founding Director, Institute on World War II and the Human Experience

This Program is Sponsored in Part by:

*The Florida State University Arts & Humanities Program Enhancement Grant
Awarded to Dr. G. Kurt Piehler*

*State Partners Grant from the Council on Culture and Art
Awarded to MoFA*

The 2015 Peace on Earth Gift

Opening Nights Festival, Chris Heacox, Director

Book Designer:
Jean D. Young, MoFA

Principal Photographers:
Jon Nalon, Tallahassee:
Florida State University Institute on World War II
Christopher White, Pensacola:
*Collections of Patrick M. Rowe—
Bill Mauldin and Design of War*

Printer:
Durra Print Inc., Tallahassee, FL

Bill Mauldin Artworks
© Bill Mauldin
Courtesy of Bill Mauldin Estate LLC

© 2015
Florida State University Museum of Fine Arts
College of Fine Arts
All Rights Reserved
ISBN 978-1-889282-30-5

THE HUMAN EXPERIENCE

TABLE OF CONTENTS

Sponsorship and Organization..2

Acknowledgments & World War II Writers' Weekend
G. Kurt Piehler..5

The Collections of the Institute on World War II and the Human Experience: Memory, Remembrance, History
G. Kurt Piehler & Richard Siegler..7

Artifact Identifications from the Institute
Anne Marsh, Sharyn Heiland Shields, Luke Cochran..2-91

The Oliver L. Austin, Jr., Slide Collection: An American Ornithologist's View of Postwar US-Occupied Japan, 1946-1950
Annika Culver..29

Sgt. Bill Mauldin: Artist of the Greatest Generation
Catherine Kendall Matthews..31

The Design of War: World War II Propaganda Posters and Flags
Christina Glover...43

Notes from the Design of War Collection
Patrick M. Rowe...47

Witness to War
Christopher A. Jones..63

A Glimpse of the Collections of the Institute on World War II.............................75

Writers' Weekend Selections & Further Reading..91

Florida State University..92

Cover: Walter J. and Elaine Duggan Collection photograph with a Navy stamp on the reverse that reads: *Takeoff for Rattle, a Grumman Hellcat taking off from the* USS Lexington *somewhere in the Pacific.* The photograph was shown at the Museum of Modern Art, New York City, in 1945 in the Navy exhibition *Power in the Pacific*. Walter J. and Elaine Duggan Collection of the Institute on WWII, Florida State University.

FLORIDA STATE UNIVERSITY INSTITUTE ON WORLD WAR II

▲ *VMF 214 Swashbuckers patch*. Carl O. Dunbar Collection of the Institute on WWII, Florida State University.

▶ *Distances Sign in the Pacific Theater*. Walter J. and Elaine Duggan Collection of the Institute on WWII, Florida State University.

Elaine Duggan served in the European Theater of Operations in the Women's Army Corps while her husband Walter served as a combat photographer in the Pacific Fleet. His photographs depict an array of experiences in the Pacific Theater from the quotidian to the extraordinary: *Injured Soldiers Playing Cards* (page 87) and *Distances Sign in the Pacific Theater* are emblematic of the former, while the construction of an aircraft carrier or photos from the Japanese surrender represent the latter, unique experiences.

■ The artifacts and historic photographs of the Institute on WWII have been photographed by Jon Nalon, Tallahassee, Florida.

ACKNOWLEDGMENTS
&
WORLD WAR II WRITERS' WEEKEND

G. Kurt Piehler, PhD, Director
Institute on World War II and the Human Experience

Since 2013, the Institute has worked with two museums: first, the John and Mable Ringling Museum of Art in Sarasota, and now, with the inauguration of this exhibition, the Institute has collaborated with the Museum of Fine Arts on campus in Tallahassee. This current exhibition would not have been possible without the funding support of the University through the Arts & Humanities Enhancement Grant for research and publication and the City of Tallahassee and Leon County for community programming. The donors of The Peace on Earth Gift to the Museum have acknowledged our goals and guiding philosophy through their support, and the newly re-named Opening Nights Festival at the University has also been gracious, placing our events in the season calendar. Our grateful thanks to all.

The World War II Writers' Weekend is a free public event of talks and book signings by authors of a range of works on World War II. Speakers include Robert Gellately (*Stalin's Curse*), Michael Neiberg (*The Blood of Free Men: The Liberation of Paris*), and Whitney Bendeck (*"A" Force: The Origins of British Deception During the Second World War*). In celebration of Valentine's Day weekend, FSU student veterans will read some of the unpublished love letters of the World War II generation that are part of the collections of Florida State University's Institute on World War II and the Human Experience.

The Exhibition is comprised of separate installations brought together from generous lenders such as Dr. Patrick Rowe (*The Design of War* and the Bill Mauldin Collection) and the Oliver L. Austin, Jr., Slide Collection curated by Dr. Annika Culver, as well as selections from the Ringling Museum's Coville Collection united with photographic collections from the Institute by Curator Chris Jones to create *Witness to War*. With such fine colleagues, the Institute personnel examined the archetypal methodology and organization of many traditional museums. We had a number of questions: For instance, how can we exhibit causes, effects, and concepts by way of objects? How do we evoke the human experience of World War II through artifacts? Will the public respond favorably to our choices and interpretation? How do museums deal with contested historical issues such as repatriation of war trophies, and personal items belonging to a former enemy, such as Japanese flags embossed with the names of friends and relatives? What is the contemporary relevance and future of World War II museums?

Underlying the exhibition with its accentuation on the physical vestiges of World War II are the connections between war and society and the integration of physical objects into displays as manifestations of cultural history. Previously, many museums simply acted as repositories for disparate military hardware such as guns, uniforms, and vehicles. This exhibition seeks to integrate such materials into a larger narrative that highlights the power of an object in the context of the human experience during World War II with the hope of achieving the optimal method of extracting such power in a museum gallery.

—G.K.P.

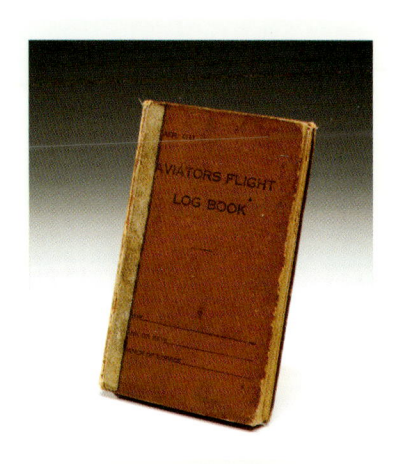

▲ *Flight Log Book*. Carl O. Dunbar Collection of the Institute on WWII, Florida State University.

Carl O. Dunbar, a pilot, entered the US Naval Reserve as an aviation cadet in 1941. He trained at various locations in the US before being stationed at Ewa Air Station in Hawaii. He flew with the Marine Fighting Squadron VMF-214, also known as "The Swashbucklers," who fought at Guadalcanal and the Solomon Islands, and were later renamed "The Black Sheep."

▲ *Before They Were The Black Sheep* is the story of Carl Dunbar's two-year journey through his military training and the combat missions he flew in World War II. The book is an assemblage of letters Dunbar wrote home to his family that was edited for publication by his son Peter. Carl O. Dunbar Collection of the Institute on WWII, Florida State University.

FLORIDA STATE UNIVERSITY INSTITUTE ON WORLD WAR II

▶ *Portrait of Stephen Winters, photographer.* Following WWII, Stephen Winters spent much of his career at Florida State University. His photographs are included in the *Witness to War* exhibition. Stephen Winters Collection of the Institute on WWII, Florida State University.

THE HUMAN EXPERIENCE

THE COLLECTIONS OF THE INSTITUTE ON WORLD WAR II AND THE HUMAN EXPERIENCE

Memory, Remembrance, History

G. Kurt Piehler, PhD, and Richard Siegler

Even before the guns fell silent in 1945, perceptive Americans acknowledged the magnitude of the war and sought to preserve the history of this global conflict in which the United States played a pivotal role as the "Arsenal of Democracy." Such a role was emblematic of the powerful position the nation sought to claim in international affairs. Moreover, national leaders endeavored to preserve the historical record of World War II in order to ensure that the sacrifices of this generation would be memorialized, that posterity could learn from triumphs and tragedies that resulted in the loss of millions of lives. After the Japanese attack on Pearl Harbor on December 7, 1941, President Franklin D. Roosevelt mandated that federal departments and agencies preserve the essential records of this conflict for use by future historians. Army Chief of Staff General George Marshall embraced this mandate, and the War Department drew on the talents of historians and those from other professions to document the unfolding conflict. Not content to simply rely on written records, Army historians such as the journalist S.L.A. Marshall and the professionally trained historian Forrest Pogue, who served as a sergeant, pioneered the technique of oral history. For instance, Army historians started interviewing GIs wounded during the cross-Channel assault. Wesley F. Craven, James F. Cate, Robert R. Palmer, Samuel Eliot Morison, and Bell Wiley were among the prominent historians of their era who contributed to the official histories of the Army, Navy, and Air Force.[1]

Writing and understanding the history of World War II must take into account the fact that it was a censored war. All the major combatants sought to prevent both the enemy and their own citizens from knowing the unadulterated truth about the course of the war. The Axis Powers, Germany, Italy, and Japan, did not even remotely maintain the fiction of a free press. Likewise, the Soviet Union subordinated the press to the interests of the Communist Party well before the German invasion on June 22, 1941. Such democratic societies as the United States, Great Britain, and Canada restricted the flow of information to the public. American journalists stationed with American forces were required to obtain military credentials and had to submit their stories for censorship. There were important military secrets that were essential to keep private, especially the dates of impending invasions, code breaking capabilities, and military strength. At the same time, censorship allowed government officials to manipulate the public and hide incompetence and questionable decisions. For instance, the American public was shielded from accurate information on the attack on Pearl Harbor for nearly a year even though the Japanese knew full well the destruction they had wrought on the American battle fleet.[2]

▲ *Stephen Winters standing with camera* (*inscription*: "I'm shootin' into the sun..."), gelatin silver print. Stephen Winters Collection of the Institute on WWII, Florida State University.

▲ *Charlotte Mansfield, photographer.* Charlotte Mansfield Collection of the Institute on WWII, Florida State University.

---

1 Wesley F. Craven and James F. Cate, *The Army Air Force in World War II*, 7 vols. (Chicago: University of Chicago Press, 1948-1958); Samuel Eliot Morison, *History of US Naval Operations in World War II*, 15 vols. (Boston: Little, Brown, 1947-1962); and Robert R. Palmer, Bell I. Wiley and William R. Keast, *The Procurement and Training of Ground Combat Troops* (Washington, DC: Historical Division, Department of the Army, 1948).

2 Philip Knightley, *The First Casualty: From Crimea to Vietnam: The War Correspondent as Hero, Propagandist, and Myth Maker* (New York: Harcourt Brace Jovanovich, 1975), 271-273.

FLORIDA STATE UNIVERSITY INSTITUTE ON WORLD WAR II

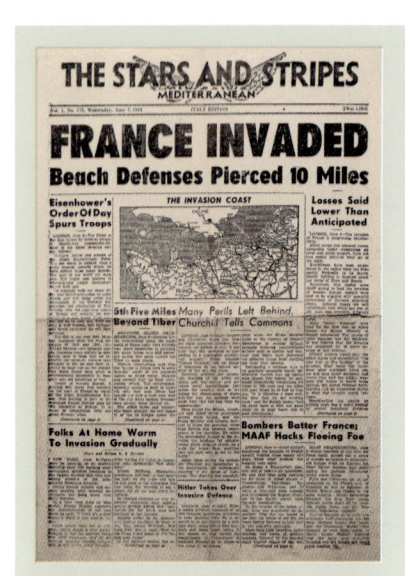

▲ *The Stars and Stripes* issues of June 7, 1944, and April 8, 1945. Collection of Patrick M. Rowe.

▶ *Ulm, Germany.* Charlotte Mansfield Collection of the Institute on WWII, Florida State University.

THE HUMAN EXPERIENCE

Despite these restrictions, American journalists wrote the first version of historical events, and World War II produced some of the finest journalistic accounts ever written about war. William Shirer (1904-1993), present at many of the key events in this conflict, including the French surrender to Adolf Hitler in June 1940, would write one of the first major authoritative accounts of the war, *The Rise and Fall of the Third Reich* that would sell millions of copies after it was published in 1960. Ernie Pyle (1900-1945) famously avoided reporting on senior political and military leaders. Instead, he sought to focus on the experiences of average GIs, especially those on the front line. A trademark of his columns, among the most widely syndicated during the war, would be listing the home addresses of the men, and sometimes women, he wrote about.[3]

The US Army supported a sophisticated GI written and edited newspaper, *The Stars and Stripes*, and magazine, *Yank*. *The Stars and Stripes* was granted a heretofore unprecedented degree of journalistic freedom and often earned the ire of some generals, most notably US Army General George Patton. Some of the most prominent journalists of the postwar era, including Andy Rooney (1922-2011), staffed *The Stars and Stripes*. Bill Mauldin (1921-2003), who began his career with a National Guard unit, became the most famous cartoonist during the war through his caricatures of two weather-beaten and grimy infantrymen, Willie and Joe.

Journalists were not the only ones to write early drafts of the history of the war. Virtually all GIs wrote to someone on the home front telling them about their experiences, both quotidian and sensational. Millions of letters were written, and they conveyed information on both the most significant and mundane aspects of the war. GIs wrote about journeys across the United States for training as individuals and as parts of a unit, hazardous journeys across the high seas, and the experiences in foreign lands. American GIs were deployed to every continent in the world, except Antarctica, and naval vessels fought on all four oceans. Officers had the further responsibility of informing and offering their condolences to the family and loved ones of the men who bravely lost their lives in the line of duty.

The letters of GIs were censored, and many that survive bear the mark of censors who clipped out portions of letters that offered information regarding an individual's location, prospective mission, or other details that would potentially aid the enemy. Additionally, the institutionalization of censorship by the United States military encouraged self-censorship among servicemen. Many GIs knew that others aside from the intended recipients were going to scrutinize their correspondence. The grim nature of war itself also encouraged self-censorship since many GIs deliberately sought to hide the gruesome nature of war from their families and friends. The breezy quality of many letters belie a war that often produced staggering casualties for those engaged in front line combat on land, sea, or in air.

Yet censorship could be evaded. Many GIs and their families devised codes that allowed them to communicate more freely, including where they were and when they were to see combat. Against regulations, many GIs did keep diaries to record their experiences, and they often conveyed a far different account of the war than was offered in news reports and media accounts. Censorship not only applied to journalists and GI letters, but a tight control was also placed on images released to the public. Photographs showing the gore of the battlefield ended up not in the front page of newspapers, but in the secret files of the War Department. The content that Americans saw on the newsreels and documentaries was assiduously restricted. For several years, the Roosevelt Administration refused to allow images of dead GIs to be released to the public. Only later in the war did the government relent out of fear

▲ *The Stars and Stripes* issues of April 13 and May 8, 1945. Collection of Patrick M. Rowe.

---

[3] For a comprehensive anthology of American journalism during the war, see *Reporting World War II*, 2 vols. (New York: Library of America, 1995).

FLORIDA STATE UNIVERSITY INSTITUTE ON WORLD WAR II

▲ *United States Flag*, January, 1944. United States Navy Ensign. *Inscription*: US ENSIGN / NO 9 / MARE ISLAND / JAN 1944 (along the hoist of the flag [i.e., the border of the flag nearest to the flagpole]). Collection of Patrick M. Rowe.

▶ *7th WAR LOAN / NOW..ALL TOGETHER*. 1945. *Artist*: from a painting by C.C. Beall that was based on an Associated Press photograph by Joe Rosenthal. Collection of Patrick M. Rowe.

THE HUMAN EXPERIENCE

the American home front had grown complacent and needed to be reminded of the sacrifices made by GIs.[4]

Fortunately, many uncensored images of the war survived the conflict, and they offer an important counterpoint to the photographs that were published in *Life* magazine and other news periodicals. Combat photographers serving with the armed forces, and photojournalists, retained images that were not published and brought them home after the war. Often, against explicit orders, GIs carried cameras with them; their photographic record provides a less sanitized version of daily life on duty.

Censorship in the United States ended with victory, but self-censorship endured. Many GIs who had been away from home, in some cases for as long as five years, were eager to get on with their lives. Like veterans of earlier conflicts, most of the GIs leaving the military did not join a veteran's organization. In contrast to World War I, the Spanish American War, and the Civil War, GI Joe statues did not sprout on town squares and in front of county courthouses. Instead, the generation that returned from this global war favored "living memorials" that improved the quality of life in their communities. Hospitals, parks, stadiums, playgrounds, schools, and community centers were among the living memorials favored by veterans and their communities in the 1940s and 1950s. In contrast to the often, "mediocre or even tawdry monumental monstrosities that have been left in the wake of all our earlier wars," as one critic put it, these living memorials had a truly social purpose that best honored the memory of the fallen.[5]

Interestingly, it was not the traditional monuments of stock statues of GI Joe or conventional granite markers noting those who had fallen that preserved and commemorated World War II in the popular mindset.[6] Rather, newspaper photographs, newsreels, motion pictures, television, and later museum exhibits, captivated the country.

The preeminent example of the dynamism of newspaper photographs is Joe Rosenthal's (1911-2006) dramatic picture depicting five marines and a Navy medic raising an American flag on Mount Suribachi on February 23, 1945, during the battle for Iwo Jima. This image became one of the most popular symbols of the American war effort during the Second World War and embodied the heroism, bravery, and courage of a nation in arms. Its widespread adoration resulted in Congress swiftly passing legislation which authorized the building of a permanent monument to memorialize the flag-raising on Iwo Jima.

When GIs began to return home, many said little about their war experiences to parents, spouses, and children. A few brought home war trophies, like Japanese rifles and bayonets, and stories to accompany the artifacts. In some cases, they believed that they had simply done what was expected of them, an emblematic sign of the patriotism that was commonplace among the World War II generation, to a large degree. In a society that numbered 139.93 million in 1945, over sixteen million men and women served in the armed forces.[7] For the generation that came of age during the 1920s and 1930s, military service remained the norm. Of those who did not wear a uniform, many either held essential positions in war industries or were disqualified as a result of physical or mental disabilities.

A multitude of veterans remained silent as a result of the trauma of war. To cope, many buried their memories and concentrated on jobs, families, and their community.

▲ Peter Sanfilippo paintings *Enemy Under Attack*, *Arab Mountain Troops*, and *Fallen Friend*. Peter Sanfilippo Collection of the Institute on WWII, Florida State University.

Peter Sanfilippo enlisted in the Army on November 5, 1941, after which he was sent to North Africa. He was actively involved in transporting heavy guns in the 633rd Field Artillery, 5th Army.

Sanfilippo's unit moved from North Africa into Sicily and up through Italy. As a method of coping with the stress of war, Sanfilippo painted watercolors of what he witnessed. He painted events and scenes as they happened, using a German ammunition box as an easel. If circumstances demanded a quick exit, his fellow soldiers would help him pack his paintings, by rolling them up and stuffing them into empty shell casings to be sent home. Sanfilippo was honorably discharged at Fort Dix, New Jersey, on August 26, 1945.

---

4 George H. Roeder, Jr., *The Censored War: American Visual Experience During World War Two* (New Haven, CT: Yale University Press, 1993).
5 G. Kurt Piehler, *Remembering War the American Way* (Washington, DC: Smithsonian Books, 1995), 134.
6 Piehler, *Remembering War the American Way*, 135.
7 Department of Veteran's Affairs, "America's Wars," United States Department of Veteran's Affairs, May, 2013, accessed 5 September 2014, http://www.va.gov/opa/publications/factsheets/fs_americas_wars.pdf.

▶ *Escape map*. James E. Flynn Collection of the Institute on WWII, Florida State University.

Escape maps developed during World War II were printed on double-sided fabric. They were often carried by many American and British servicemen in case they were held as POWs behind enemy lines. The maps could be used without making any noise, and they could be hidden inside uniforms that would not betray their existence during a POW inspection.

The cloth maps could also be used to patch clothes, filter water, make a sling or a bandage and could also serve as a handkerchief.

James Flynn, from Butte, Montana, was a flight engineer who flew bombing missions on both B-25 and B-29 aircraft in North Africa, the China-India-Burma theater and in the Pacific. Flynn's map shows the Eastern Portion of Kunming, Yunnan, China to Chabua, Assam, India while the reverse shows the Western Portion of the same locale.

On the first side of the map, there are translations of a message from English to the six languages spoken in that region. The message says:

"I am an American airman. My plane is destroyed. I cannot speak your language. I am an enemy of the Japanese. Please give me food and take me to the nearest Allied military post. You will be rewarded."

▶ *Japanese armband*. Brokaw / Richard L. Shively Collection of the Institute on WWII, Florida State University.

Richard L. Shively was trained as a bombardier at the Great Lakes and in San Diego and served at Midway and Guadalcanal in the Pacific. He earned the Purple Heart and Silver Star, awarded for valor after being shot three times by a Japanese floatplane.

Shively's items came to the Institute on World War II as part of the Tom Brokaw Collection. The Japanese armband is a relic Shively retrieved from combat with Japanese forces on the Lunga River on Guadalcanal in 1942. The flag on the left represented the Japanese Navy while the flag on the right was the Japanese National flag. The Japanese calligraphy on the left means "bravery," while that on the right signifies "loyalty."

THE HUMAN EXPERIENCE

Others turned to alcohol as the drug of choice to cope with the stress of war and postwar life. At the time, post-traumatic stress disorder was not recognized by military doctors, limiting the treatments available to veterans, including therapy. Only as they reached their sixties and seventies did many World War II veterans feel comfortable sharing their stories with oral historians. In a war in which much could not be written down or was lost, the testimony of individuals fulfills a crucial role in understanding the history of World War II.

As the years following World War II came and went, a multitude of veterans were increasingly willing to divulge their stories. Retirement and the sense of their own mortality encouraged many to grapple with the remarkable events of their youth. In addition, grandchildren often expressed an interest in the artifacts of their grandfathers, such as the uniforms and letters found while clearing out attics and basements. They also found interested audiences for their stories and receptivity that was unthinkable during the tumultuous 1960s. The senior leaders of the Vietnam War were World War II veterans, and the term "Greatest Generation" was the last label such leaders could have expected to be bestowed amid widespread anti-war sentiments. In the 1980s, popular mini-series like Herman Wouk's "Winds of War" (1983) captivated Americans and renewed interest in the conflict: so, too, did the 1984 D-Day Anniversary. By the 1990s, the passions surrounding the Vietnam War that had so divided the World War II generation from the Baby Boomers had cooled. The work that helped define this new appreciation of the World War II generation was Tom Brokaw's book *The Greatest Generation* (1998).

The Institute on World War II and the Human Experience, founded in 1997 through Florida State University's Department of History, emerged out of this wave of popular interest to preserve the human dimension of the Second World War. Despite voluminous writings on the campaigns of that war and on the major personalities of the time, the war's profound impact on the individual American man and woman had largely been left uncharted by the end of the 20th century. The primary *raison d'être* of the Institute is to rectify that deficiency and provide a centralized collection for research on questions related to the human experience of World War II. The first collection that heralded the foundation of the Institute, that of Paul K. Dougherty, a photographer with General George Patton's Third Army, was destined for the fate of obscurity, and even worse, disposal, that is until his son, Kevin Dougherty, realized its tremendous worth as a piece of the historical record and individual memory of the war. He offered his father's photographs, some of which included the liberation of the concentration camp at Dachau, to the Institute's original director, the late Dr. William Oldson. Six months later, Dr. Oldson received a phone call from George Langford who was interested in donating documents relating to his service in World War II in the 20th Armored Division, as well as those relating to the service of his two brothers and sister. The Dougherty and Langford collections are two pillars upon which the Institute's foundation rest; these collections were the catalyst for Dr. Oldson to begin collecting the documents from every man and women who served the nation abroad or on the home front. What began as a personal endeavor to save pieces of history has become a public archive dedicated to the preservation of a myriad of intimate memories and the record of human experience during World War II.

In 2001, the generosity of Tom Brokaw endowed the Institute with a plethora of items that had been sent to him while he was writing his trilogy on the "Greatest Generation." One such item is a distinct Japanese cloth armband (facing page). As a whole, the Institute embodies the often complex task of memorializing such a vast and profoundly intense conflict, utilizing both physical objects as well as oral histories. The variety of paper objects (artifacts) held in the Institute's collections include letters, newsletters, diaries, official documentation, memoirs, books, periodicals, posters, poetry, artwork, vinyl records, maps, and photographs. Furthermore, the Institute

▲ *Escape maps* from the Alexander Wowk Collection and the Donald and Portia Ackerman Collection of the Institute on WWII, Florida State University.

Alexander Wowk served in the 834th Bomb Squadron and the 486th Bomb Group of the 8th Army Air Force for which he flew missions in the European Theater. On Wowk's map, Sheet E is for servicemen who might find themselves in Germany, the Protectorate of Bohemia and Moravia, Slovakia, Poland and Hungary.

Donald Ackerman was stationed in England with the 44th Bomb Squadron, 506th Bomb Group, 8th Air Force and flew 17 missions. After the war, Ackerman was stationed in Nagoya, Japan, during the Allied Occupation.

13

FLORIDA STATE UNIVERSITY INSTITUTE ON WORLD WAR II

▲*Prisoner of war exchange near Lorient, France*, November 1944, gelatin silver prints. Paul K. Dougherty Collection of the Institute on WWII, Florida State University.

▶*Entrance to Dachau*, 1945. Paul K. Dougherty Collection of the Institute on WWII, Florida State University.

Technical Sergeant Paul K. Dougherty was a photographer for the US Army who captured the quotidian life of fellow soldiers as they went through basic training in Tallahassee, Florida. Dougherty and his future wife met at the Tallahassee USO and would often enjoy lunch together at the Sweet Shop. After his training at Dale Mabry Field, Dougherty became the official Army photographer of General George S. Patton's campaign through Europe. Dougherty's work leaves little to the imagination and illustrates the powerful human narrative that was World War II. This image is of the entrance to Dachau Concentration Camp in Germany where 27,839 men and women were killed before the Allies liberated the camp in 1945.

THE HUMAN EXPERIENCE

also houses a substantial assortment of three-dimensional objects including uniforms from all of the military branches, the GI's standard equipment, helmets from a variety of nationalities including American, German, and French, Bibles, a pair of Japanese Navy binoculars, cloth escape maps, K-Ration kits, flags, German cigarette card books, medals, and a wide variety of memorabilia, to name but a few items. Some of these were kept by US soldiers as souvenirs of their enemy on the battlefield.

As the Institute has grown out of founding director Dr. Oldson's desire to preserve the physical record and memory of World War II and its veterans, the ever-relevant question of what to accept into the collection has remained central to its direction in the last seventeen years. Since the collection is currently housed on the top floor of the Bellamy building, there is limited space, particularly in terms of storing physical artifacts. There are two questions that are central to the continued development of the Institute's collection: What objects are most crucial to understanding the human dimensions of World War II and should be prioritized for preservation? Where does the meaning and importance of objects accepted in the collection originate? Ideally, decisions are made on a case by case basis with a thorough inspection of the item's history, its condition, and its potential as a tool of learning through its fundamental relationship to the legacy of World War II. Materials that epitomize the daily life, the humor, and the heartache of human experiences both during and after the war have been mainstays in the collection. Thus, the Institute has had to think long and hard about what objects and documentation are essential to memorializing the war and the brave men and women who fought in it.

The Arsenal of Democracy

The United States was the last major power to enter the war in late 1941. Although the dominant memory of World War II within American society is that it was the "good or morally necessary conflict," it was a controversial war prior to Pearl Harbor. Americans were deeply divided on how to respond to the rise of fascist Italy, Nazi Germany, and Imperial Japan. When Japan invaded Manchuria in 1931, the United States Government issued protests and condemned the 1932 establishment of the Manchukuo puppet state, but took no measures to either rearm or place economic sanctions against Tokyo. As war clouds gathered in Europe in the 1930s, the United States Congress bowed to public pressure to forestall American involvement in another war by passing a series of Neutrality Acts.

When Germany invaded Poland on September 1, 1939, few Americans wanted to or expected to join the conflict. Even the precipitous fall of France in June 1940, failed to convince the majority of Americans that the United States would fight another land war in Europe. Nonetheless, the fall of France alarmed President Franklin D. Roosevelt (FDR) and incited him to oversee an unprecedented military buildup through vastly increased defense spending, the enactment of conscription, and the federalization of the National Guard. Roosevelt sided with Great Britain in 1940 and thus abandoned any pretense of neutrality. Using executive action, FDR provided Britain with US destroyers in return for the right to build American military bases in British territory in the Western Hemisphere.

In his radio address delivered from Washington, DC, on December 29, 1940, FDR called on America to become the "great Arsenal of Democracy."[8] After considerable debate, the US Congress accepted Roosevelt's call to adopt the Lend Lease program, by providing aid to Great Britain, and later, the Soviet Union. Whether or not the Roosevelt administration viewed America's entrance into World War II as inevitable, the historical record offers no definitive answer. Certainly by the summer of 1941,

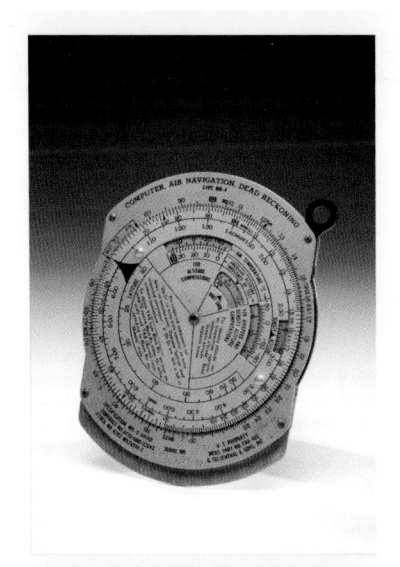

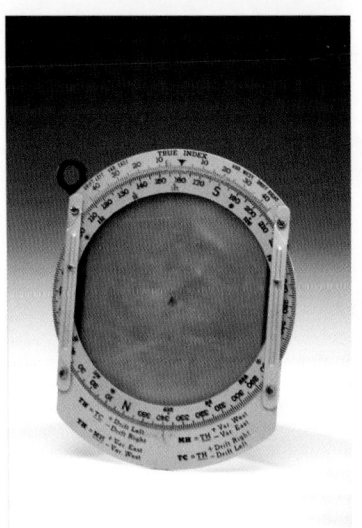

▲ *Dead reckoning device.* Donald and Portia Ackerman Collection of the Institute on WWII, Florida State University.

The dead reckoning computer was a navigational tool used in flight planning to calculate fuel burn, time en route, and wind correction. It also served to determine ground speed when in the air. This pocket-sized device was used by Donald Ackerman, who trained pilots in Marianna, Florida, to fly the P-51. He was later sent overseas as a B-24 pilot.

---
8 US, Department of State, Publication 1983, *Peace and War: United States Foreign Policy, 1931-1941* (Washington, DC: Government Printing Office, 1943), 598-607.

FLORIDA STATE UNIVERSITY INSTITUTE ON WORLD WAR II

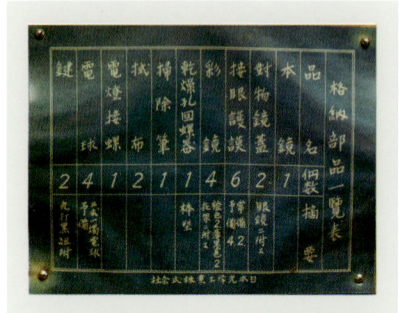

▲ *Detail from binoculars case.*

▶ *Megaphone for Japanese Civil Defense Unit, c. 1943.* Helen B. Strzelczyk Collection of the Institute on World War II, Florida State University. This megaphone originally belonged to a civil defense unit connected with a Japanese chemical plant, most likely Ishihara Industry. It was specifically intended for use by the "Fire Lieutenant of the First Group" of an auxiliary fire department created to fight fires caused by air raids. Until late 1944, Japan experienced few direct attacks and this led to complacency regarding the protection of civilians. By early 1945, the US Army Air Force regularly launched devastating air raids against Japanese cities, killing an estimated 100,000 civilians in the Tokyo fire raids of March 1945 alone. The inadequacy of Japanese civil defense measures further contributed to the loss of life.

Helen B. Strzelczyk served the Women's Army Corps in New Guinea and later the Philippines. No documentation survives on how Strzelczyk acquired this item.

▶ *Japanese binoculars and case.* George Wiszneauckas Collection of the Institute on WWII, Florida State University. The binoculars used by the Japanese Imperial Navy were produced by the Japanese Optical Industries Corporation (*Nippon Kōgaku Kōgyō Kabushikigaisha*), which is known today as Nikon. Before the development of radar later in the war, naval commanders attempting to locate the enemy typically had to rely on observations from personnel standing watch on deck or by dispatching search planes. Radio surveillance also served as another tool for trying to track the movement of the enemy fleets. The Japanese fleet heading to Hawaii in December 1941 maintained strict radio silence and this allowed it to deliver a devastating surprise attack on the American fleet anchored at Pearl Harbor.

George Wiszneauckas served with the US Army Signal Corps from 1941-1946 and participated in the campaign to liberate the Philippines. He obtained these high-powered binoculars while taking part in the Occupation of Japan.

THE HUMAN EXPERIENCE

Roosevelt declared in no uncertain terms that he wanted Nazi Germany defeated, as exemplified by joining Prime Minister Winston Churchill in issuing the Atlantic Charter. The United States by late 1941 was not only supplying goods to Britain, but the American navy was even taking part in the Battle of the Atlantic against the German navy. Even before Pearl Harbor, American forces were engaged in combat with German submarines in the North Atlantic.

GIs and the Things They Carried

The productive capacity of the United States and of its Allies is remarkable in both sheer quantity and *matériel* produced in such a short time. The United States, along with Great Britain and the Soviet Union, began to win the battle of production even before the decisive engagements at Midway (1942), El Alamein (1942), and Stalingrad (1943). The productive might of the Allies is even more impressive when one considers the fact that much of the Soviet productive capacity lay in ruins as a result of the German invasion or had been hastily relocated East to escape destruction, and Britain had to endure the destruction of the Blitz and the shortages caused by the Battle of the Atlantic. Prior to Pearl Harbor, civilian demand competed with rearmament for resources, and many businesses were reluctant to convert to military production until critical events and the federal government required them to do so.

This notion of America's incredible production capability has long been apparent in the popular mindset, emphasizing that the United States' most decisive victory in World War II was in its creation of war *matériel*. Without diminishing the sacrifices, combat prowess, and valor of the United States military during the war, the production capabilities and economic might, in terms of Gross Domestic Product (GDP), of the United States alone outstripped the combined Axis Powers and was a crucial factor in determining the war's outcome.[9] It was remarkable how rapidly the United States expanded the armed forces from less than a half million men and women in uniform in 1940, to a total strength of over fifteen million men and women by 1945.[10] The fact that they were so thoroughly supplied, both upon leaving for a front and while fighting there, was quite a feat in and of itself.[11] According to Peter Darmen, "the average American serviceman was, in the main, superbly equipped with clothing, weapons and supplies."[12] This was hardly the case during the pre-war and early-war years of World War II, a fact often overshadowed by the United States' significant contributions particularly after 1942.

The quality and quantity of equipment of the pre- and early-war United States Army can best be described as "scattershot." Much of the equipment being used consisted of holdovers from the inter-war years, remnants of World War I such as the M1917 steel helmet, and even some late 19th century articles, particularly the Winchester Model 1897 shotgun used on garrison duty. The apparent dichotomy between the superbly standardized and equipped US Army of 1943, and its previous incarnation of a hodgepodge of decades-old, mismatched equipment, is succinctly summarized by Darmen. He astutely notes that, "It is a curious fact that by the end of World War II the US Army was able to equip its soldiers with uniforms which were the most advanced in the world, but back in 1941 the uniforms worn by its personnel had appeared outdated."[13] The sheer variety of pre-war American soldiers' equipment, exemplified in Richard Windrow's *The World War II GI: US Army Uniforms, 1941-1945 in Colour*

▲ *Walkie Talkies.* The walkie-talkie, originally called a handy-talkie, was also known as the SCR-536. Developed by the predecessor of the Motorola Company, it was the smallest of Signal Corps radio and transmitter sets in World War II. The unit was battery operated with plug in crystals and coils to control the frequency of the receiver and transmitter. The antenna was a forty-inch telescoping rod that allowed the unit a range of about 1 mile over land and up to 3 miles over water. The rod also served as an on/off switch. Norm Hyne Collection of the Institute on WWII, Florida State University.

The nephew of Norm Hyne donated this walkie-talkie to the Institute on World War II after his uncle's death. Although Hyne participated in World War II, little is known of his specific service during the war.

▲ *Graflex Corp., Pacemaker Speed Graphic 4x5 camera, c. 1947* (model *c.* 1943), metal, plastic, and glass. Charlotte Mansfield Collection of the Institute on WWII, Florida State University.

---

9 Ralph Zuljan, "Allied and Axis GDP," *Articles on War* (July 1, 2003): 1, accessed 26 June 2014, http://www.onwar.com/articles/0302.htm#.
10 Morris H. Hansen, *Statistical Abstract of the United States 1943 (Sixty-Fourth Number)* (Washington: Government Printing Office, 1944), 162.
11 Peter Darmen, *Uniforms of World War II* (Edison, NJ: Chartwell Books, 1998), 55-56.
12 Ibid.
13 Darmen, *Uniforms of World War II*, 56.

▶ *Dog tags with silencer*. The dog tag is encircled with a rubber edge called a silencer, an innovation developed later in the war which prevented the dog tags, issued in pairs, from making noises as they rubbed against each other, possibly alerting a nearby enemy during field combat. Robert L. Bounds Collection of the Institute on WWII, Florida State University. Robert Bounds was inducted into the service in 1942 in Philadelphia. He had anti-aircraft training at Paris Island and was later assigned to the 5th Amphibious Division where he saw action in multiple areas of the South Pacific, most notably in the Marianna Islands from 1943-1945.

▶ *Dog tag*: P on the bottom right corner indicates *Protestant*. Lawrence Salley Stokes Collection of the Institute on WWII, Florida State University. Lawrence Stokes served in the 933rd Engineer Aviation Regiment in the US Army after training at Camp Blanding, Florida and Geiger Field, Washington. He was an Aviation Engineer in the Pacific Theater.

▶ *Dog tags*: O for blood type and *H* is for Hebrew, indicating that a soldier was Jewish. Later in the war, the *H* was changed to *J* for Jewish servicemen. Wolfson's dog tag was typical of many servicemen. Wilfred Wolfson Collection of the Institute on WWII, Florida State University. Wilfred Wolfson trained for the military in the ROTC at the University of Florida and was inducted into the US Army at Fort Bragg, North Carolina, in 1941. He served with the Army's Americal Division that reinforced the First Marine Division in combat against the Japanese Imperial Forces at Guadalcanal and for which they received a Navy Presidential Unit Citation in 1943. Wolfson eventually attained the rank of Lieutenant Colonel.

▶ *K-Rations*. The K-ration was pre-packaged individual combat food and was supplied for breakfast, lunch and dinner. The first million K-rations were ordered in May 1942, and by 1944, the peak year of production, more than 105 million rations were procured. Although the K rations were to be used for only two or three days, troops often had to rely on them for weeks at a time, and this decreased their initial popularity. P. Gordon Earhart Collection of the Institute on WWII, Florida State University. Gordon Earhart served as an infantryman and water purification specialist in the Pacific Theater. He participated in the landing at Lingayen Gulf in January of 1945 and served in the Occupation of Japan. He was discharged in February 1946 and later attended college on the GI Bill.

Photographs, dominates any study of the clothing American GIs wore during World War II. This is chiefly due to the fact that soldiers were reluctant to discard gear with which they were comfortable, unless its potential replacement had clear and numerous advantages. For instance, the Quartermaster Corps and unit officers on the front line had greater priorities than ensuring each soldier was a cookie-cutter replica by having the same model of haversack. Even if they had the desire to maintain an utterly uniform soldiery, the profusion of ever-improving equipment designs by the Quartermaster Corps, not to mention continuous shortages of various raw materials, meant that "standard" was a very fluid concept during the war.

The best the Quartermaster Corps could hope for was an approximation of a standard GI who had a rather extensive list, in comparison to other field armies, of official equipment models and designs. Not only would fabric materials such as rayon meander in and out of scarcity, resulting in different shades of the famous olive-drab color, but the Quartermaster Corps was initially dedicated to providing a standard uniform for soldiers in different branches, not to mention, unique clothing which was required for the variety of climates an American soldier might be fighting in. This inventory of climatic military garbs put the Army Quartermaster department, "under increasing pressure to standardize its fighting ensemble and dispense with the multitude of outfits being developed and stocked for special-purpose troops."[14] The result was the creation of the M1943 combat uniform, the purpose of which was to establish a standard combat uniform in place of the numerous specialized combat clothing being worn by infantry, armored troops, paratroopers, and mountain troops.[15]

Military personnel on the home front tested the M1943 experimental combat uniform in a variety of climate zones and daily activities under normal and harsh conditions. While the M1943 experimental uniform was ultimately judged to be unsatisfactory for army-wide implementation, many of its components were refined and later formed the basis of several standard items, particularly the "rugged jungle pack." Shelby Stanton argues that, "In many respects, the M1943 experimental combat outfit was one of the most important army uniform projects of World War II."[16] Furthermore, the desire for innovation and improvement within the Army's Quartermaster Corps contrasted starkly with the respective corps of other armies during World War II. This desire is highlighted by the military's application of its energies into designing a system of military combat clothing that "would be comfortable, hard-wearing, and suitable to the needs of the soldier in all the different climatic regions in which he might be called upon to fight."[17] This policy of striving for comfort was not without its critics, none more so than Allied European officers who, "considered the comparatively comfortable American shirt and trouser combination too leisurely and sometimes derided it as 'golfing' clothes."[18] Nevertheless, the successive articles of the uniform that were approved for individual use became extraordinarily popular among the soldiery, particularly in the European Theater of Operations, where the uniform was worn extensively.

The official uniform gradually achieved a semblance of standardization after 1943 as pre- and early-war equipment became worn-out, outdated, and phased out of active service. Despite that, there remained one area of a soldier's load that was never standardized: the unofficial things he carried. In this case, "unofficial" is best defined as articles of clothing, equipment, or personal items that are not standard issue, but are worn or carried by choice of the individual soldier. Common to most American soldiers was paper and a pen to write home to loved ones, and photographs of family or loved ones. Bibles or other religious texts and articles such as rosaries, crosses, and prayer

▲*Coleridge Augustus Jemmott*. C.A. Jemmott was inducted into the US Army at Cambridge, Massachusetts in 1942. He served with the "I" Company of the 22nd Quartermaster Regiment in Africa and Italy. One of his duties was to assist with the transport of the giant German railway cannon named "Anzio Annie" after it was sabotaged and abandoned by German forces. He was discharged with the rank of Sergeant in 1945. Coleridge Augustus Jemmott Collection of the Institute on WWII, Florida State University.

▲*Lt. James S. Bowns on Jeep*, Paris, 1944 or 1945, gelatin silver print. James S. Bowns Collection of the Institute on WWII, Florida State University.

---

14 Capt. Shelby L. Stanton, *US Army Uniforms of World War II* (Mechanicsburg, PA: Stackpole Books, 1994), 82.
15 Richard Windrow, *The World War II GI: US Army Uniforms 1941-45 in Colour Photographs* (Wiltshire, UK: The Crowood Press UK, 2008), 84.
16 Stanton, *US Army Uniforms of World War II*, 85.
17 Windrow, *The World War II GI: US Army Uniforms 1941-45 in Colour Photographs*, 4.
18 Stanton, *US Army Uniforms of World War II*, 37.

COMMON CLOTHING	WEIGHT IN POUNDS
Underwear	.43
Socks	.19
Long Johns	2.24
Pants & Shirt, Wool	2.82
Pants Belt, with Buckle	.19
Knit Cap	.13
Field Boots, M1943 (10-inch)	4.38
Sweater, Wool	1.12
Field Trousers, M1943	2.00
Field Jacket, M1943	3.30
Parka (Raincoat/Poncho Equivalent)	2.81
Scarf, Wool	.41
Gloves, Wool	.13
Socks, Extra	.19
Blanket, Wool	3.69
Shelterhalf, Canvas	4.50
Personal Items	1.90
TOTAL WEIGHT	**30.43**

EQUIPMENT	WEIGHT IN POUNDS
M1 Helmet, with Liner	3.19
First Aid Pouch, M1942	.40
Canteen, M1910	7.38
Entrenching Tool, M1943	2.94
Suspenders, M1936	.95
Field Bag, M1936	1.81
K-Ration, 3 Meals	2.31
Gas Mask with Carrier, M9	4.00
TOTAL WEIGHT	**22.98**

EQUIPMENT, RIFLEMEN	WEIGHT IN POUNDS
Rifle, M1 Garand	10.20 (Loaded)
Sling, M1	.53
Cleaning Kit, M1	.53
Cartridge Belt, M1923	1.44
Ammo: 10 x 8-Round Clips	5.31 (In Cartridge Belt)
Ammo: Bandolier with 6 x 8-Round Clips (x2)	6.74 (3.37 Each)
Bayonet, M1 with M7 Scabbard	1.56
Grenade, MK II Frag. (x2)	2.62 (1.31 Each)
Hatchet, M1910	1.50 (est.)
Pistol	2.00 (est.)
TOTAL WEIGHT	**32.43**
Common Clothing	30.43
Common Equipment	22.98
RIFLEMEN'S COMBAT LOAD	**85.84 LBS**

▲ *Gas mask made in the United States*, probably around 1943, by the Mine Safety Appliances Company (MSA) in Pittsburgh, Pennsylvania. It is the second version of the US M1-1-5 Optical Gas Mask and was made in very limited quantities primarily for service personnel who had to use optical equipment during a gas attack. Snipers and Ships Captains would have carried this type of mask. William Byrd Collection of the Institute on WWII, Florida State University. William Byrd was working in Jacksonville, Florida, for Railway Express when he left in 1943 to join the US Marine Corps. He was trained at Parris Island in South Carolina, Camp LeJeune in North Carolina, San Diego, and Camp Catlin in Hawaii. He served as a radar operator primarily in Okinawa. He was discharged from the US Marine Corps in March of 1946.

▲ *Folding trench shovel with pick*. The folding shovel/pick combination, of the type seen here, was designed in 1945 but was not produced on a wide scale before the war ended. Many shovels were retrofitted with the pick assembly so shovels with earlier production dates are often found with a pick. This shovel does not have a production date or place imprinted on it. Lloyd McDuffie Hicks, Jr., Collection of the Institute on WWII, Florida State University. Lloyd Hicks, of Bradenton, Florida, completed Officer Candidate School in 1942, and training at the Armored Forces
[continued in sidebar page 21]

books served to sustain the spirit of many troops under harsh conditions. Soldiers with a religious affiliation were also granted permission to have the letters P (Protestant), C (Catholic), or H (Hebrew) stamped onto their dog tags for use in case of death so that a proper burial could be performed.[19] The use of such letters is clearly illustrated by the dog tags of Lawrence Salley Stokes and Wilfred W. Wolfson.

Other ubiquitous items included wallets, toiletries, and personal care items. Finally, soldiers stationed in different theaters and cities acquired a cornucopia of items ranging from tourist souvenirs to materials captured from the enemy. For example, such novelties included privately purchased goods such as roller-bar belt fasteners, hair brushes, spectacles, eye-droppers, jewelry in the form of watches or rings, playing cards, maps, and cases for compasses or binoculars. In addition, they may have carried supplementary gunny sacks, ammunition packs, or bandoliers, trigger-finger mitten shells, and a wide range of other items that added to the already considerable weight soldiers carried during World War II. On page 20 is a list of the average combat load of a World War II US soldier in the winter of 1944-45, courtesy of LTC Hugh F. Foster (Ret.) of the 45th Infantry Division.[20]

Adequately supplying the American GIs with durable, climate-oriented, and comfortable articles of clothing was a struggle for the Quartermaster Corps during the first three years of World War II, but properly outfitting the Women's Army Corps (WAC) beginning on July 1, 1943, was a distinct challenge. The Quartermaster Corps found itself in a predicament, where timely provisioning was of the essence: "The establishment of the Women's Army Auxiliary Corps (WAAC) in early 1942, expanded and re-designated as the Women's Army Corps (WAC) during September 1943, was an unexpected development that caught the Quartermaster Corps unprepared to produce suitable wartime clothing for women quickly."[21] With over 140,000 women serving in the WAAC/WAC during World War II, large quantities of women's clothing were required in a relatively short period of time to properly outfit these women for service. The WACs were dispersed widely across the globe, serving in locations such as New Guinea, Manila, Leyte, and Hollandia, New Caledonia, India, North Africa, and the European Theater of Operations, including General Dwight Eisenhower's headquarters.[22]

Initially, the men of the Quartermaster Corps took the lead in designing uniforms for the Women's Army Corps, minimizing gender distinctions at the expense of comfort. However, that decision quickly turned into an abject disaster as they "tried to design a WAAC uniform based on men's standard sizes, such as 42 long, 42 short, etc., whereas women's sizes were entirely different. The result was a stiff and masculine looking uniform."[23] Moreover, this cavalier response did little to quell concerns that focused on the potentially dangerous "masculinizing effect the Army might have on women, and especially on the disruptive influence the WAC would have on sexual standards."[24] Many of the women subjected to wearing the provided, masculine clothing often had to walk a tightrope and "negotiate within cultural and medical frameworks that viewed their desires to enter the Army and their role within the WAC as possible evidence of lesbianism."[25] The WAVES (Women Accepted for Volunteer Emergency Service), who were the naval counterpart to the WAC, handled the task of uniform design more

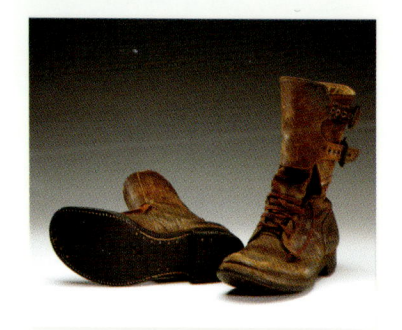

School at Fort Knox, Kentucky, where he received special instruction in the Gunnery Department in the use and repair of weapons. He became a liaison officer with the famed 2nd Armored Division, 41st Armored Infantry Regiment and took part in the Battle for France in 1944. For meritorious service during that time he was awarded the Bronze Star.

▲ *Leather boots.* The design of these well-worn double buckle M43 combat boots evolved from the former service shoes used with leggings. The M43 or "Boots, Service, Combat" became the first true combat boot, made by extending the service shoe with a high top cuff that closed by a pair of buckles and straps as seen here. The higher top replaced the leggings, a great simplification of both supply and combat use. The boots had a one-piece sole and heel made of molded synthetic or reclaimed rubber. The new boots were developed as part of the M1943 field uniforms authorized in November 1943. They were not issued to many troops until late in World War II, and then issued only to overseas units. Troops usually wore their trousers tucked into the tops of their M43s. Bob Sabaroff Collection of the Institute on WWII, Florida State University. Bob Sabaroff was inducted into the Army in June of 1944 and received basic training at the Infantry Replacement Training Center. He served with Company K, 271st Infantry Regiment, 69th Division and fought at the Battle of the Bulge. His division later broke the Siegfried Line and made its way into Germany. Sabaroff was discharged on January 15, 1946.

---

19 Paul F. Braddock, *Dog Tags: American Military Identification Tag 1861 to 2002* (Chicora, PA: Mechling Publishing, 2003), 143.
20 LTC Hugh F. Foster III, "The Infantry Soldier's Load, Winter of 1944-45," *45th Infantry Division*, last modified 24 February 2010, accessed 5 September 2014, http://www.45thdivision.org/Pictures/General_Knowlege/combatload.htm.
21 Stanton, *US Army Uniforms of World War II*, 211.
22 Jill Halcomb Smith, *Dressed for Duty: America's Women in Uniform, 1898-1973* (San Jose, CA: R. James Bender, 2003), 308.
23 Smith, *Dressed for Duty: America's Women in Uniform, 1898-1973*, 315.
24 Leisa D. Meyer, *Creating GI Jane: Sexuality in the Women's Army Corps During World War II* (New York: Columbia University Press, 1998), 153.
25 Ibid.

FLORIDA STATE UNIVERSITY INSTITUTE ON WORLD WAR II

▲ ▶ *Margaritte Ivory-Bertram and nurses' class photo.* Margaritte Ivory-Bertram became a member of the first group of African American nurses commissioned by the US Army Nurse Corps at Fort Bragg, North Carolina in 1941. After basic training at Bragg, she was assigned to duty in Liberia, West Africa, where she served as a ward nurse, mess officer and night supervisor; she achieved the rank of 1st Lieutenant Chief Nurse.

While serving in West Africa, Bertram contracted malaria and suffered prolonged complications from it. Near the end of the war, she returned to Fort Bragg where she cared for the wounded from the D-Day invasion at Normandy. She was discharged from the Nurse Corps in 1945. Gertrude Margaritte Ivory-Bertram Collection of the Institute on WWII, Florida State University.

▲ *Division sweetheart charm bracelet.* Chaloupka Collection of the Institute on WWII, Florida State University.

▶ *WAC in uniform with luggage*, 1944, gelatin silver print. Charlotte Mansfield Collection of the Institute on WWII, Florida State University.

delicately. Navy women were able to purchase their uniforms and be individually fitted for them in direct contrast to those women serving in the Army.[26]

Surprisingly, the US Army's Quartermaster Corps had consulted several industry experts, but ultimately, failed to create a satisfactory line of clothing that suited the WAC for dress, field, and working purposes. These lamentable issues were only resolved as the Quartermaster Corps branched out of its comfort zone and sought the assistance of female designers and the head of the WAC, Colonel Oveta Culp Hobby. Of further concern were the procurement setbacks that hampered the supply line for both GIs and WACs during the early years of the war. Many WACs were forced through basic training without uniforms, and those who did have uniforms were often just wearing makeshift approximations until the real ones arrived.[27] While these conditions may have seemed challenging, considering the early problems of production across many military supply wares, Smith argues that it was really a matter of Quartermasters overlooking the particular needs of women: "The whole problem of supply to the WAC can be traced to the seeming lack of interest on behalf of the Quartermaster Corps of the Army, the Requirements Division and the Services of Supply."[28] This notion is further reinforced by Stanton, who alludes to the fact that a women's clothing section did not even exist in the Quartermaster's research and development branch until the last year of the war.[29] Quite obviously, it was given a distinctly low priority.

Eventually, standard issue materials began to filter into the WAC training locations with barracks bags, utility bags or purses, collar insignia, sets of sewn-on rank and other sleeve insignia, enlisted overcoats, scarves, blouses, skirts, garrison caps, shirtwaists, gloves, identification tags, anklets, leather lace-up wooden boots, stockings, neckties, underwear, towels, and toiletries being distributed amongst the women. The core of the uniform consisted of six-gore skirts and single-breasted jackets with four pockets and a self-belt, "primarily fabricated from materials, such as heavy canvas and haircloth that proved completely unsuitable for proper fitting."[30] Although the women were not directly involved in combat formations, proper clothing was especially crucial as the war progressed, and female specialists, as well as nurses, were placed in advanced positions under battle conditions. In the North African and early Italian campaigns, women's work garments were still unavailable, and they were forced to work in men's jackets, herringbone twill suits, and boots. This was far from ideal because "the unsatisfactory sizing differences often caused discomfort, difficulties in duty performance, and less than ideal protection against wind or adverse weather."[31] This completely unsuitable women's uniform design, first introduced in July, 1942 to the WAAC personnel at Fort Des Moines, Iowa, received immediate criticism from the public. Unfortunately, the uniform deficiencies were not rectified until well into the war, and after a series of extensive pattern revisions. It was a constant work-in-progress and a regrettable testament to the trial by error method adopted by a military unused to the presence of women serving in war.

Unofficially, women often sustained themselves by carrying items similar to their male counterparts. Faith was a strong element among the WACs with many of the enlisted members carrying one or more of the following objects: rosaries, crosses, Hebrew Bibles, Christian Bibles, and prayer books. Women's private possessions corresponded with those of GIs, with a fair number of them constituting tourist souvenirs and personal items. Some of the plentiful examples include coin purses, handkerchiefs, matchbooks, wallets, sewing kits, guide books, songbooks, cameras, glasses, brushes, pillows, scissors,

▲ Photograph inscription reads *"Rita Strobel — I think, 1944 or 1945,"* gelatin silver print. Charlotte Mansfield Collection of the Institute on WWII, Florida State University.

▲ *Willie Mae Williams*, of Hillsborough County, Florida, was inducted into the Women's Army Corps in April 1943 after completing high school. Trained as a cook at Ft. Devens, Massachusetts, she learned to prepare special diet meals for recovering wounded and sick patients. Her tours of duty took her to military hospitals at Fort Des Moines, Iowa and later Camp Muskogee, Oklahoma. She was discharged with the rank of Private First Class in 1945. Willie Mae Williams Collection of the Institute on WWII, Florida State University.

---

26 Meyer, *Creating GI Jane: Sexuality in the Women's Army Corps During World War II*, 154.
27 Ibid.
28 Smith, *Dressed for Duty: America's Women in Uniform, 1898-1973*, 315-316.
29 Stanton, *US Army Uniforms of World War II*, 211.
30 Ibid.
31 Stanton, *US Army Uniforms of World War II*, 212.

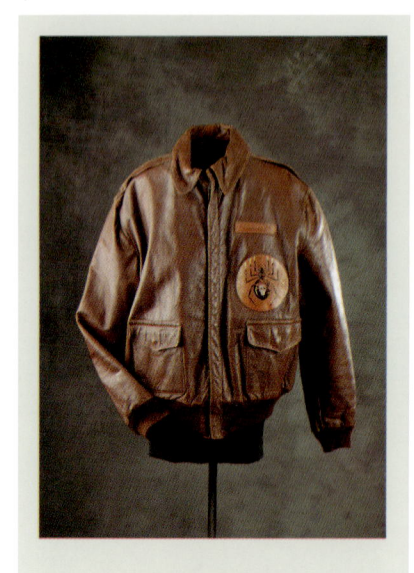

FLORIDA STATE UNIVERSITY INSTITUTE ON WORLD WAR II

▲ *Aviator jacket with spider drawn on it.* Perry E. Hudson Collection of the Institute on WWII, Florida State University.

Perry E. Hudson was inducted into the Army Air Corps in August 1942. He received pilot training in Texas and became a night fighter instructor in California and Florida. Hudson's aviator jacket sports the insignia of the black widow spider, the symbol of the P-61 Northrup Night Fighter aircraft known as the "Black Widow."

▶ *WACs stand at attention for review by Queen Elizabeth*, 1944 or 1945, gelatin silver print. Charlotte Mansfield Collection of the Institute on WWII, Florida State University.

▶ *Major Watkin's Crew*, 405th Bomb Squadron, 38th Bomb Group, *c.* 1943-1944, gelatin silver print. Gordon McCraw Collection of the Institute on WWII, Florida State University.

THE HUMAN EXPERIENCE

can openers, dictionaries, leggings, and insect repellent sticks. Overall, the GIs and WACs possessed quite similar items that sustained morale, were acquired, or were issued during the war.

Other branches of the armed forces of the United States had distinctive uniforms that had practical functions, but also sought to inculcate and promote shared values. The stark contrast between the dress uniforms of the Navy, in their dapper "Full Dress" whites and the Marines in their smart "Blue Dress," is emblematic of the singularity each branch sought in respect to its role in the larger military apparatus. Not to be outdone, the pilots, navigators, bombardiers, and other air corps flyers of the Air Force sported the comfortable and practical Type A-2 leather flight jacket. Aside from famously customizing their aircraft with elaborate nose-art, members of the Air Force also personalized their jackets with elaborate symbols and colorful designs. The time spent adding intricate details demonstrated the pride they took in wearing what became a unique identifier and a treasured article of their uniform. The A-2 was just as much a symbol that personified an airman as a distinct member of the armed forces as his beloved wings. One of the specialized items some of these airmen carried were escape or evasion maps printed on fabric that were used to guide servicemen to safety from behind enemy lines. While actions and purview of the different branches of the armed forces notably divided servicemen, they were also physically distinguishable through the uniforms they wore and the equipment they carried from Western Europe to the Pacific Ocean.

A Global War from an American Perspective

As part of the Grand Alliance with Great Britain and the Soviet Union, the United States played an essential role in defeating the Axis Powers. American productive capacity not only supplied American forces, but proved vital to the British and Soviet forces as well. In contrast to the Soviet Union which refused to divide its attention between Nazi Germany and Imperial Japan (except for the last week of the Pacific War), the United States fought a two-front war in both Europe and the Pacific. When the Western Allies stormed ashore on the five beaches in Normandy, the American forces made up sixty percent of the 175,000 Allied forces taking part in the invasion. British manpower would steadily shrink in the final year of the war, and the strains of war became even more apparent for this island nation and empire engaged in fighting since 1939.

The United States could not have won World War II without its Allies. In neither Europe nor the Pacific did the United States have to confront alone the bulk of Axis forces. In the struggle against Nazi Germany, the Soviet Union fought the majority of Hitler's forces from June 1941, until V-Day in May 1945. The Soviet Union lost twenty-six million killed in the Great Patriotic War. The United States casualties, while not insignificant, paled in comparison. Over 400,000 Americans died in this conflict, far higher than any single conflict since the American Civil War. However, if the United States had had casualty numbers rivaling the Soviet Union, would posterity be inclined to label it the Good War?

In the struggle against Imperial Japan from 1937-1945, Chinese forces confronted the bulk of Tokyo's forces. Outside of China, Allies such as Australia in New Guinea and the British and Indian forces in Burma proved crucial in turning the tide of war. Even though the United States emerged as the dominant naval force in the Pacific against the Japanese navy, it depended on British and Canadian navies bearing the brunt of the Battle of the Atlantic. American GIs were well aware of the role of their Allies. When surveyed by Samuel Stouffer's team of social scientists during the war, average GIs serving in Europe expressed admiration for the role played by Soviet forces.

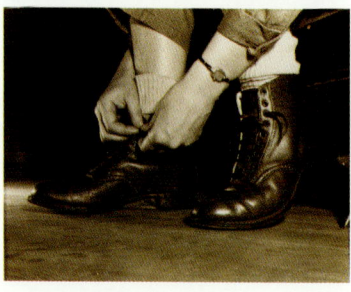

▲ *Nurse cape*: the Navy nurse's cape of June Husband Harrison, made of heavy wool, was distributed by the Naval Uniform Shop at the Navy Clothing Depot in Brooklyn, New York. It has a velvet collar with a dark maroon lining. The "frog" closure differs from the more commonly used double placket with buttons. June Harrison served in the US Navy as a nurse during World War II from 1943 to 1946. She was inducted at Farragut, Idaho, and discharged at McAlester, Oklahoma; Harrison ultimately achieved the rank of Lieutenant (jg). June Husband Harrison Collection of the Institute on WWII, Florida State University.

▲ *"They break down my ankles, spread my feet and don't feel so good—but I still love 'em,"* c. 1943-1945, gelatin silver print. Charlotte Mansfield Collection of the Institute on WWII, Florida State University.

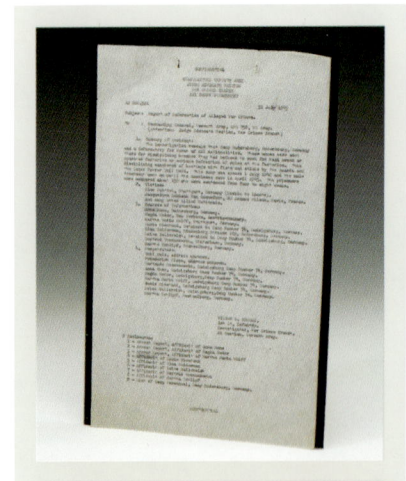

FLORIDA STATE UNIVERSITY INSTITUTE ON WORLD WAR II

▲ *Nuremberg documents*: original documents from records of the Nuremberg trials. Wilson Brooks Collection of the Institute on WWII, Florida State University.

Wilson Brooks enlisted in the US Army at Camp Blanding, Florida in February 1941. He became a Warrant Officer and served in the 42nd Infantry Division in the European Theater; Brooks participated in the Battle of the Bulge and took part in the liberation of the Dachau Concentration Camp. As a Warrant Officer, Brooks conducted investigations for the trial of Nazi perpetrators held at Nuremberg, Germany.

▶ 486th Bombardment Group, 3rd Wing, 8th Air Force. *Scenes of the aftermath of German bombing in London*, 1944-1945, gelatin silver prints, SN11332.411 and SN11332.414. Gift of Warren J. and Margot Coville. Collection of The John and Mable Ringling Museum of Art, the State Art Museum of Florida, Florida State University, Sarasota, Florida.

THE HUMAN EXPERIENCE

The human experience of World War II was definitively novel and global in character. Most of the Americans who fought in World War II had never flown in an airplane, traveled abroad, and had seldom left their home states. World War II sent GIs to the four corners of the world, and in some cases, men and women were deployed first to Europe and later to Asia. They encountered cultures with differing linguistic, political, religious, and cultural traditions and interacted with men and women of different ethnic and racial backgrounds. Personnel deployed to Asia and Africa encountered societies that were part of wider empires and witnessed the impact of colonialism on indigenous peoples.

Thus, it follows that the memorialization of World War II is a widespread phenomenon with countries across the globe choosing to remember it in manifold ways. One common method among North Americans, Europeans, and Australians was to use museums to commemorate their respective involvement in the wars, and to illustrate, through documents and physical objects, war's impact on the experience of individuals. According to Philip Karl Lundeberg, "The essential mission of military museums in the United States remains teaching through the study and interpretation of historical artifacts, first exemplified at America's oldest armed forces museum, the Musée d'Artillerie (1843) at West Point."[32] Dissimilar to the centralized war museums that can be found across European capitals, American military museums and locations are dispersed throughout the nation, commonly at battlefields, seaports, fortifications, or military bases. Furthermore, the United States boasts numerous private and state-owned museums that reflect the widespread public admiration for the armed forces and their role in the nation's development.

Following in this extensive lineage of World War II museum exhibitions, the intended goal of twenty-first century approaches is to highlight the personal and human experiences of a wide range of military personnel and civilians who were thrust into a global conflict of unparalleled scale and scope. Underlying this exhibition are connections between war and society and material culture that are exemplified through the integration of physical objects as manifestations of cultural history. We of the Institute on World War II and the Museum of Fine Arts at Florida State University hope that this larger, global narrative will reveal the power of the object in the context of the human experience of war and that such individual stories will interest visitors of all ages.

G. Kurt Piehler is Director of the Institute on World War II and the Human Experience and Associate Professor of History at Florida State University. He is the author of *Remembering War the American Way* (2004) and editor of the *Encyclopedia of Military Science* (2011). As founding director (1994-1998) of the Rutgers Oral History Archives of World War II, he interviewed over 200 veterans from the World War II generation. He is currently writing a monograph examining the religious life of the American GI in World War II.

Richard J. Siegler is a Master's student with the Department of History at Florida State University and a member of the Institute on Napoleon and the French Revolution. He is currently writing his MA thesis, which will be defended in the spring of 2015, entitled: "The Official Word, From Consulate to Hereditary Empire: Political Justification and Explanation for Significant Shifts in Domestic Napoleonic Politics, 1799-1815."

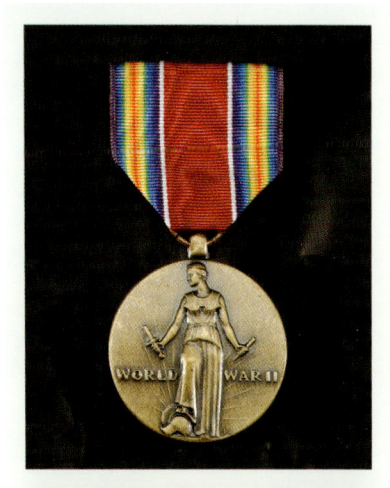

---

32 Paul Karl Lundeberg, "Museums, Military History" in John Whiteclay Chambers, ed., *The Oxford Companion to American Military History* (New York: Oxford University Press, 2000), 456.

▲ *Victory Medal*, front and back. William Markovich Collection of the Institute on WWII, Florida State University.

The Victory Medal was authorized by an Act of Congress on July 6, 1945, and awarded to all members of the Armed Forces who served at least one day of honorable, active federal service between December 7, 1941, and December 31, 1946. The front of the medal depicts the personification of Liberty while the reverse contains the words, "FREEDOM FROM FEAR AND WANT, FREEDOM OF SPEECH AND RELIGION, and UNITED STATES OF AMERICA 1941-1945." The red center stripe of the ribbon is symbolic of Mars, the Roman God of War, representing both courage and fortitude. The twin rainbow stripes, suggested by the World War I Victory Medal, allude to the peace following a storm. A narrow white stripe separates the center red stripe from each rainbow pattern on both sides of the ribbon.

▲ Austin often went specimen-collecting in the countryside while observing the state of Japan's wildlife and forests, but as a talented photographer, he shot more than just birds. This rural family in Japan lined up by the side of the road to look at the curiosity of the American ornithologist passing by poignantly expresses both their hope in a better postwar future, but also threadbare weariness of over a decade of deprivation. One sees the abundance of crops and the seeming pride of the young man behind the fence. Oliver L. Austin, Jr., Collection of the Institute on WWII, Florida State University.

▶ Marquis Hachisuka and the gulls. Marquis Hachisuka Masauji (1903-1953), a Cambridge-trained Japanese aristocrat and one of Japan's leading ornithologists, developed a close professional relationship with Dr. Austin, accompanying him on many trips to collect specimens throughout Japan to gauge the effects of the war on the diversity of Japan's bird and mammal species. The Austin boys enjoyed swimming in his naturally-heated outdoor pool in his palatial French Riviera-style villa in Atami; SCAP had requisitioned his Tokyo mansion which later became the Australian Embassy. Here, Hachisuka appears in a gull rookery, dwarfed and surrounded by a healthy colony. However, almost eight years of total war (1937-1945) ravaged Japanese mammal populations and song birds, which were caught in mist nets and sold as food. Yakitori ("roast bird"), or a popular snack of roasted chicken on skewers, was originally made with songbirds since late feudal times, until Dr. Austin stopped the practice for conservation purposes.

▶ White Horses. In January 1950, the Austin family was invited to the Imperial Palace for a farewell party by Crown Prince Akihito, who is depicted folding his hands behind his back, in a characteristic pose. Much to the consternation of their mother Elizabeth, both Tony and Timmy Austin briefly rode on one of the imperial white horses, made famous in the US by images of Emperor Hirohito's wartime steed Shirayuki (who died in 1947). Tony had served as an English conversation partner to the Crown Prince; the boys regularly enjoyed games of bridge and Monopoly.

THE OLIVER L. AUSTIN, JR., SLIDE COLLECTION

An American Ornithologist's View of Postwar US-Occupied Japan, 1946-1950

Annika Culver, PhD

Dr. Oliver L Austin, Jr., headed the Wildlife Branch of the Fisheries Division in the Natural Resources Section (NRS) for SCAP (Supreme Commander for the Allied Powers) from September 4, 1946, to December 31, 1949. He was honored as one of only two members of the US Occupation of Japan who received a personal commendation for meritorious civilian service from General Douglas MacArthur.

Austin implemented reforms of game laws and created wildlife sanctuaries as well as public hunting grounds to help conserve and manage Japan's wildlife and natural resources.

During his nearly four years in Japan, Austin left behind almost 1,000 well preserved color photographic slides of postwar Japan under reconstruction: highlights include American expatriate life, ordinary Japanese families in Tokyo and the countryside, and Japanese veterans purveying street entertainments. The images reveal high artistic quality and composition while they provide a glimpse into an important era in US-Japan relations.

Through his ornithological connections, Austin met and collaborated with deposed Japanese aristocrats who engaged in the study of birds as connoisseurs or as researchers, including Prince Takatsukasa, head priest of the Meiji Shrine. He also collaborated with Marquis Yamashina Yoshimaro, founder of the Yamashina Institute for Ornithology. Austin's son Tony—who served as the conversational English partner of Crown Prince Akihito, the current Emperor of Japan — donated this remarkable collection which features rare color photographs of Emperor Akihito as a youth, scenes of the grounds of the imperial palace, and shots of collateral members of the imperial family.

With the acquisition of the Austin collection, the Institute now houses the largest extant collection of Occupation Era color images in the United States, Japan, or anywhere else, composed of nearly 1,000 slides of photographs taken between 1946-1950. As depicted in his photographs with scientific precision, ornithologist Dr. Austin was working for SCAP (Supreme Commander of the Allied Powers) on Japan's postwar wildlife and conservation policies, and his impressions as a scientist show unique views of Japanese society from the aristocratic elite down to ordinary rural folk, while highlights include rare views of teenaged boys from the Japanese imperial family interacting with their American counterparts. In a broader sense for scholarship in the Japanese and American studies fields, the digital archive features environmental history, postwar social change, political revival, and items of anthropological interest (depictions of traditional Japanese festivals and rural folklife).

Annika Culver is an Assistant Professor of East Asian History at Florida State University and serves as Faculty Consultant (East Asia) for the Institute on World War II and the Human Experience. She curates the Oliver L. Austin, Jr., Photographic Collection, a digital collection of US Occupation-Era images of postwar Japan, and researches visual and literary cultures of Japanese imperialism, having recently published *Glorify the Empire: Japanese Avant-Garde Propaganda in Manchukuo*.

Dr. Oliver L. Austin, Jr.

Recipient of the first doctorate in ornithology from Harvard University in 1929, Austin was a world renowned authority on birds in the twentieth century. After serving in World War II, he was posted in Korea, and then, in occupied Japan to head the Natural Resources Section. In Tokyo, Austin met Japan's leading ornithologists, including Yamashina Yoshimaro and Hachisuka Masauji. Austin later published *Birds of Japan* (1953) with Baron Kuroda Nagahisa (1916-2009). Before his death, Dr. Austin served as Curator Emeritus of Ornithology at the Florida Museum of Natural History and retired in Gainesville, Florida. Oliver L. Austin, Jr., Collection of the Institute on WWII, Florida State University.

Yamashina Yoshimaro

Marquis Yamashina Yoshimaro (1900-1989), originally an imperial family prince and a politician in the postwar Japanese Diet's House of Peers, pioneered the modern study of ornithology in Japan. In 1932, he founded the Yamashina Institute for Ornithology in his Tokyo estate in the Shibuya district. In early Spring 1945 US Army Air Corps air raids destroyed his home, but spared specimen collections and laboratories housed in his museum (its aviary inhabitants had already perished from wartime starvation).

Yamashina's contribution as a scientist included using cytology to categorize birds, especially ducks, and in postwar Japan, he researched poultry breeding to feed a protein-starved population. In a requisitioned villa, Dr. Austin revived meetings of the Chôgakkai (Bird Society) that Yamashina had founded in the prewar period. This image shows Yamashina with two of his specimens that had miraculously survived wartime conflagration. Oliver L. Austin, Jr., Collection of the Institute on WWII, Florida State University.

FLORIDA STATE UNIVERSITY INSTITUTE ON WORLD WAR II

Artwork identifications by Patrick M. Rowe.

▪ Bill Mauldin Collection of Patrick M. Rowe photographed by Christopher White, Pensacola, Florida.

▶ Printed cartoon published in *The Stars and Stripes*, Mediterranean edition, signed *Bill Mauldin* (lower right; signed in the plate), Saturday, July 1, 1944. Copyright 1944 by Bill Mauldin. Courtesy of Bill Mauldin Estate LLC. Notes: Mauldin's favorite cartoon characters during World War II were Willie and Joe. In this full-page illustration from *The Stars and Stripes*, Joe is shown in the background smoking a cigarette and holding a lit match while Willie is in the foreground holding a pencil, reckoning on a calendar how many days they have been in combat. Although Mauldin modified the appearance of Willie and Joe over time, how they appear in this illustration is the way they were most commonly depicted. Joe is shown with a rounded nose and eyes that create the appearance of stress and fatigue. Willie has a square jaw and a hooked nose. Typically, both are unwashed, unkempt, and have scruffy beards.—PMR

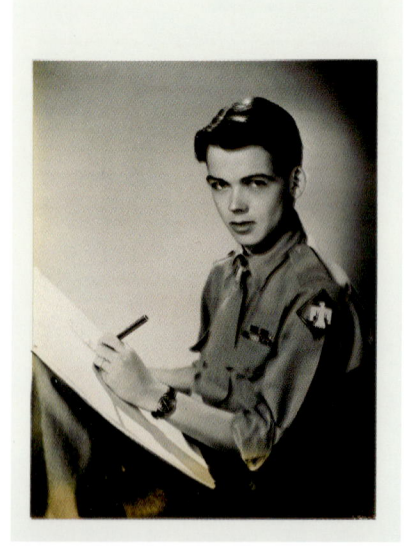

SELECTIONS FROM THE COLLECTION OF DR. PATRICK M. ROWE

SGT. BILL MAULDIN

Artist of the Greatest Generation

Catherine Kendall Matthews

During the Second World War, the United States military turned the country's youth into soldiers in a matter of weeks. Then the war, all too often, turned their wives into widows. Few were able to express all that these men had seen and faced in such a short time as clearly as Willie and Joe, the creations of cartoonist Bill Mauldin. These two GIs knew exactly what needed to be said and exactly how to say it. They were born fully formed, disgruntled, with clever banter and three-day-old beards. Mired in filth, this pair of "dogfaces" voiced the thoughts of more than a million men, inked, printed, and published for an entire country to read. In the simplest words, these fictional personae told the raw truth that outraged, uplifted, and educated the world on the truth of life in combat. For civilians and soldiers alike, Willie and Joe represented the American combat infantrymen of World War II.[1]

Acknowledging the simple brilliance of Mauldin's work, *New York Times* book reviewer Charles Poore wrote that this cartoonist "has told more people what the soldier really thinks about war than all our living poets." Later, Poore would acclaim Bill Mauldin as the most important illustrator of his age, "one whose words and pictures had shaped the nation's wartime consciousness." Living the life himself, Mauldin was able to capture the essence of the American soldier during World War II. With wry commentary depicting the daily life of the ordinary soldier, Mauldin mixed humorous quips, lively sarcasm, and veiled meanings within his illustrations. They made fun of officials, regulations, and the monotonous but deadly routine of the infantrymen. Beneath many of the jokes, however, lay serious criticism and a pile of grievances toward all who were not on the front line with them. These simple yet captivating cartoons expressed the GI's frustration with officers, government officials, and even the American public.

Born on October 29, 1921, and raised in the rural southwest, Bill Mauldin was accustomed to hardship. As a consequence of the poverty of the Great Depression, young Bill was deprived of proper nutrition as an infant, resulting in a case of rickets. According to his family, however, he was never discouraged by his physical problems. "There are sinkers and there are swimmers. Apparently, I decided to thrash around," Mauldin mused years later. Bill was young, reckless and, due to his rickets, had a small, awkward physique. Sensitive about his presumed lack of strength from his softened bones and stunted growth, Mauldin thrived on a thirst for recognition. While a juvenile, Bill ended up "starting more fights than anybody else and winning none of them." Eventually, Mauldin would turn to his greatest natural talent: drawing. His style of drawing stemmed from the only idea of art Mauldin knew as a child, the illustrations in 1930s popular magazines and newspapers. He would spend his nights honing his drafting skills until daybreak and became determined to achieve a successful artistic career. In 1939, the seventeen-year-old Mauldin enrolled at the Chicago Academy of

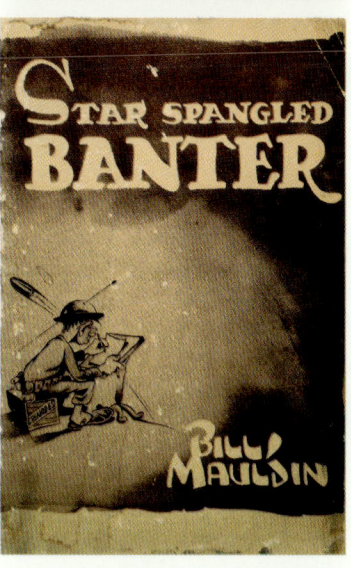

By kind permission of the Estate, photo-reproductions of artworks created by Bill Mauldin that are in the Rowe Collection appear courtesy of Bill Mauldin Estate LLC.

---

1 The most current information on the life of Bill Mauldin is recorded in Todd DePastino, *Bill Mauldin: A Life Up Front* (New York: W. W. Norton, 2008). For Bill Mauldin's description of his World War II experiences, see Bill Mauldin, *Up Front* (New York: Holt and Co., 1945). For a comprehensive catalogue of Bill Mauldin's World War II cartoons and descriptive information about them, see Todd DePastino, ed. *Willie and Joe: the WWII Years*. 2 vols. (Seattle: Fantagraphics, 2008).

FLORIDA STATE UNIVERSITY INSTITUTE ON WORLD WAR II

▶Top left: *"Expectin' rain?"* Printed cartoon: *Up Front With Mauldin* published in the *Daily News*, Los Angeles, California, signed *Bill Mauldin* (lower left; signed in the plate), Tuesday, January 16, 1945 (previously published in *The Stars and Stripes*, Mediterranean edition, October 31, 1944). Copyright 1945 by Bill Mauldin. Courtesy of Bill Mauldin Estate LLC.

▶Top right: *"Th' socks ain't dry yet, but we kin take in th' cigarets."* Printed cartoon: *Up Front With Mauldin* published in the *Daily News*, Los Angeles, California, signed *Bill Mauldin* (lower left; signed in the plate), Wednesday, January 31, 1945 (previously published in *The Stars and Stripes*, Mediterranean edition, December 14, 1944). Copyright 1944 by Bill Mauldin. Courtesy of Bill Mauldin Estate LLC.

▶Lower left: *""Sir, do ya hafta draw fire while yer inspirin' us?"* Printed cartoon: *Up Front / By Mauldin* (published in *The Stars and Stripes*, Mediterranean edition), signed *Bill Mauldin* (lower right; signed in the plate), Wednesday, December 13, 1944. Copyright 1944 by Bill Mauldin. Courtesy of Bill Mauldin Estate LLC.

▶Lower right: *"I'm beginnin' to feel like a fugitive from th' law of averages."* Printed cartoon: *Up Front With Mauldin* published in the *Daily News*, Los Angeles, California, no signature, Wednesday, January 24, 1945 (previously published in *The Stars and Stripes*, Mediterranean edition, November 2, 1944). Copyright 1944 by Bill Mauldin. Courtesy of Bill Mauldin Estate LLC.

Fine Arts and began studying to be a full-time cartoonist. Able to purchase only one year of tuition, Mauldin, quite confidently, did not expect to need further training. One professor had claimed that his "ignorance is complicated by cockiness," but the wildly ambitious Mauldin refused to let criticism discourage him.

Artistic success for Mauldin did not develop overnight. After his laborious stay in Chicago, Mauldin turned back to one of his childhood aspirations, to join the military. Mauldin had always had a fondness for tales of military adventure and had spent much of his youth listening to war stories from his Pop and Uncle Billy. So when an old ROTC friend, Jack Heinz, came to persuade him to join the Arizona National Guard, it did not take much encouragement. Mauldin strongly agreed that the United States should go to the aid of Great Britain and Western Europe in their struggle against Hitler's Germany. The Nazis had invaded Poland a year earlier, had just conquered France, and it appeared as though Britain was next in line. Bill knew that the US would eventually be drawn into the conflict. Standing 5'10" and weighing 110 pounds, the eighteen-year-old was much lighter than the minimum weight requirement that was soon to be mandated for army recruits. So on September 12, 1940, when Mauldin was sworn in as an enlisted soldier, it was only four short days before the new mandate took effect; he was assigned to the 45th Infantry Division in the United States Army. Had Mauldin made the decision to join the army only a week later, his military career might never have occurred, and his voluminous work from World War II might never have been created. "I had a crazy notion in the back of my head," Mauldin recalled years later, "that maybe there would be some way in which I could combine my artistic and soldierly talents."

Sketchbook in hand, the new recruit searched every opportunity for artistic inspiration. While in the 45th Infantry Division, he eagerly volunteered his time to illustrate for the unit's newspaper. Eventually, two of his early characters morphed into the iconic figures America now recognizes as Willie and Joe, who, subsequently, became synonymous with the average American GI. During Mauldin's initial days as an artist in the military, Joe was depicted as a cheeky, bold Choctaw Indian with a hooked nose, and Willie was shown as his red-necked sidekick. In addition, the two characters were somewhat better groomed in the early days, and Mauldin's commentary focused on less controversial aspects of military life — but as the war matured, so did Bill and his characters. Mauldin pointed out that he even switched the soldiers' names in mid-career, explaining in his book *Bill Mauldin's Army* that the two characters "matured overseas during the stresses of shot, shell, and K-rations, and grew whiskers because shaving water was scarce in mountain foxholes, and for some reason Joe seemed to become more of a Willie and Willie more of a Joe."

In July 1943, Mauldin, as a sergeant in the 45th Division's Press Corps, arrived at the front during the invasion of Sicily. He found himself one of many soldiers involved in Operation Husky, which at the time was the largest amphibious invasion in history. Part of the American Seventh Army, the 45th Division was to aid in protecting the British left flank until the entire island was liberated. Even in actual combat, Mauldin was determined to continue his documentary of the fighting soldier. Bill and fellow editor of the 45th Division news, Don Robinson, forged their way through unknown Italian territory, jumping ahead of the front lines in search of a local print shop to produce a newspaper for the troops. Mauldin continued to draw and print for the Division's newspaper during the Italian campaign. It was during this period that Mauldin's cartoons practically dripped with disdain and sarcasm, revealing his uncertainty toward combat, regulations, and officers, while simultaneously offering humorous, morale-boosting anecdotes for the common infantryman.

Many of his drawings, like Mauldin himself, were full of dark and critical thoughts protected by the shield of humor used by men who knew that most of their friends, and possibly themselves, would not survive the war. Joking was a part of coping, a way to make light of the situation and to get their minds off the horrific reality of

▲ *The Prince and the Pauper*, printed cartoon: *Up Front…By Mauldin* published in *The Stars and Stripes*, Mediterranean edition, signed *Bill Mauldin* (lower right; signed in the plate), Monday, February 28, 1944. Copyright 1944 by Bill Mauldin. Courtesy of Bill Mauldin Estate LLC.

▲ Printed cartoon: *Up Front With Mauldin* published in *The Seattle Star*, signed *Bill Mauldin* (lower right; signed in the plate), c. July 15, 1944 (previously published in *The Stars and Stripes*, Mediterranean edition, May 12, 1944). Copyright 1944 by Bill Mauldin. Courtesy of Bill Mauldin Estate LLC.

FLORIDA STATE UNIVERSITY INSTITUTE ON WORLD WAR II

▶Top left: *"I brung ya a chaser for all that plasma, Joe."* Printed cartoon: *Up Front…By Mauldin* published in *The Stars and Stripes*, Mediterranean edition, signed *Bill Mauldin* (lower right; signed in the plate), Saturday, July 1, 1944. Copyright 1944 by Bill Mauldin. Courtesy of Bill Mauldin Estate LLC.

▶Top right: *"Just gimme a coupla aspirin. I already got a Purple Heart."* Printed cartoon: *Up Front…By Mauldin* published in *The Stars and Stripes*, Mediterranean edition, signed *Bill Mauldin* (lower left; signed in the plate), Saturday, July 8, 1944. Copyright 1944 by Bill Mauldin. Courtesy of Bill Mauldin Estate LLC.

▶Lower left: *NEWS ITEM; WASHINGTON—A special badge will be awarded to Army medical personnel who served under fire.* Printed cartoon: *Up Front With Mauldin* published in *The Seattle Star*, signed *Bill Mauldin* (lower right; signed in the plate), *c.* March 1945 (previously published in *The Stars and Stripes*, Mediterranean edition, March 6, 1945). Copyright 1945 by Bill Mauldin. Courtesy of Bill Mauldin Estate LLC.

▶Lower right: *"Can't ya read signs?"* Printed cartoon: *SWEATIN' IT OUT….By Mauldin*, signed *Bill Mauldin* (lower left; signed in the plate), *c.* September 11, 1945. Copyright 1945 by Bill Mauldin. Courtesy of Bill Mauldin Estate LLC. Notes: One of the many causes that Bill Mauldin championed was civil rights. Others of Mauldin's cartoons demonstrate that as early as World War II he objected to discrimination against minorities. Another of his cartoons, which is viewed by many as the most memorable cartoon in the history of the United States, is meant to illustrate the grief the country was feeling as a result of the assassination of President John F. Kennedy. That cartoon shows Abraham Lincoln, the great President and advocate of civil rights, expressing his sorrow after hearing of Kennedy's assassination. —PMR

34

their predicament. This reality was a far stretch from the pristine images the War Department was releasing to the American public at the time. Newsreels and posters depicted spotless, well-rested soldiers brimming with confidence in final victory. These "shiny" soldiers the government wanted in public view were often nothing like the real American soldier who spent his days lying in the mud, counting the hours, and praying to survive. The real soldiers carried with them the baggage and distress of combat, but many officers and most civilians were unaware of the men's suffering or, even worse, indifferent toward it. Still, Mauldin aimed to depict reality in his cartoons, and these disgruntled, dirty combat infantrymen were just the men needed to produce a body of hard-hitting satires that would engage a nation.

Bill Mauldin quickly became an expert in producing and portraying these images. Because of his popularity with the GIs, in February 1944 he was officially transferred to *The Stars and Stripes*, the newspaper for the entire American armed forces. Bill's cartoons were now able to reach all soldiers in both the European and Pacific Theaters, and within a month his illustrations and life story would flood across newsstands back in the United States. Ernie Pyle, the most popular and influential war reporter of the time, remarked "Bill Mauldin appears to us over here to be the finest cartoonist the war has produced. And that's not merely because his cartoons are funny, but because they are also terribly grim and real. Mauldin's cartoons aren't about training-camp life…They are about the men in the line — the tiny percentage of our vast army who are actually up there in that other world doing the dying. His cartoons are about the war." Mauldin would later comment about other artists' war cartoons saying, "Like the magazine's staff itself, these cartoon characters were in the army, but not of it," showing Mauldin's readers that he, unlike the artists back in the States, did not just sit in a cubicle with a pen and paper playing make-believe, imagining the thoughts of soldiers. Mauldin had even been awarded the Purple Heart, having been wounded in the shoulder by German mortar fire while visiting a machine gun crew near Monte Cassino in September of 1943.

Bill Mauldin lived and breathed the military life like his front line comrades and the characters, Willie and Joe. Mauldin never let infantry equipment or uniform be inaccurately depicted. An old-fashioned flat World War I helmet or a Springfield rifle would never be depicted in a Mauldin cartoon where more modern equipment was in fact appropriate. He believed that the details of description were hugely important to the validity of his cartoons and, compared to the imagery in the cartoons created by artists not participating in the war, Mauldin made sure that everything was accurately rendered and placed in the correct setting. Before long, with help from Ernie Pyle, newspaper, magazine, and book editors began publishing Mauldin's panels. The American public received their first taste of Mauldin's bittersweet parodies and would not be able to get enough of his authentic work.

Many high-ranking officers in the Army, however, were offended by Mauldin's satires. They objected to his portrayal of unclean, unshaven soldiers who had attitudes often bordering on insubordination. In fact, one of Mauldin's cartoons in particular mocked the absurd demand that all soldiers must be clean-shaven at all times, even in combat. In response to Mauldin's cartoons, General George S. Patton, Jr., commander of the Third Army, threatened to cut off the newspaper's circulation to his troops. The General, well known for his strict, traditional military views, claimed that Mauldin was spreading discontent with his depictions of "grimy characters" who "had no respect for the army, their officers, or themselves." Patton had howled at Bill, "What are you trying to do…incite a goddamn mutiny?" Being the quick-witted jokester that he was, after being asked what he thought of the meeting with the General, Mauldin had simply replied that it was "as if I were hearing Michelangelo on painting." Eventually, General Dwight Eisenhower, Supreme Allied Commander in Europe, stepped forward and forced Patton to back down in his dispute with Mauldin. Eisenhower wisely realized

▲ "Brave Man," printed cartoon: *Up Front with Mauldin* (published in *The Seattle Star*), not signed, c. April, 1945 (previously published in *The Stars and Stripes*, Mediterranean edition, April 20, 1945). Copyright 1945 by Bill Mauldin. Courtesy of Bill Mauldin Estate LLC. Notes: What Bill Mauldin was to cartooning during the war, Ernie Pyle was to journalism. Like Mauldin, Pyle was not satisfied to sit behind a desk, always working a safe distance behind the front lines. Both men felt it was important to be "up front" in order to fully understand the realities of the war. In addition, Pyle, like Mauldin, worked in a style that was not pretentious, but instead direct and genuine. More than anyone, it was Ernie Pyle who brought attention to the artistic talents of Bill Mauldin. In one of his articles, Pyle wrote the following about Mauldin:

BILL MAULDIN, CARTOONIST IN ITALY, January 15, 1944-

Mauldin's cartoons in a way are bitter. His work is so mature that I had pictured him as a man approaching middle age. Yet he is only twenty-two, and he looks even younger…His maturity comes simply from a native understanding of things, and from being a soldier himself for a long time. He has been in the Army three and a half years.

It was primarily because of Ernie Pyle that Mauldin's cartoons were syndicated in newspapers across the United States. Unfortunately, Ernie Pyle was killed by a sniper's bullet during the Battle of Okinawa. He died on April 18, 1945, around four months before the end of the war. As a tribute to his friend, Bill Mauldin published this cartoon. —PMR

FLORIDA STATE UNIVERSITY INSTITUTE ON WORLD WAR II

▶ Top left: *"Radio the old man we'll be late on account of a thousand-mile detour."* Newspaper with a printed cartoon: *Up Front With Mauldin* published in *The Stars and Stripes*, Liege edition; Vol. 1, No. 82, signed *Bill Mauldin* (lower right; signed in the plate), Wednesday, April 11, 1945 (this cartoon was previously published in *The Stars and Stripes*, Mediterranean edition, February 21, 1945). Copyright 1945 by Bill Mauldin. Courtesy of Bill Mauldin Estate LLC.

▶ Top right: *"Beautiful view! Is there one for the enlisted men?"* Printed cartoon: *Up Front With Mauldin* published in the *Daily News*, Los Angeles, California, signed *Bill Mauldin* (lower center; signed in the plate), Thursday, November 2, 1944 (previously published in *The Stars and Stripes*, Mediterranean edition, September 25, 1944). Copyright 1944 by Bill Mauldin. Courtesy of Bill Mauldin Estate LLC.

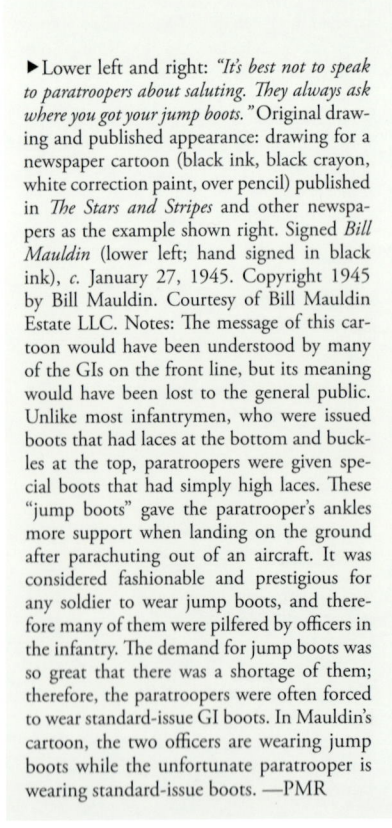

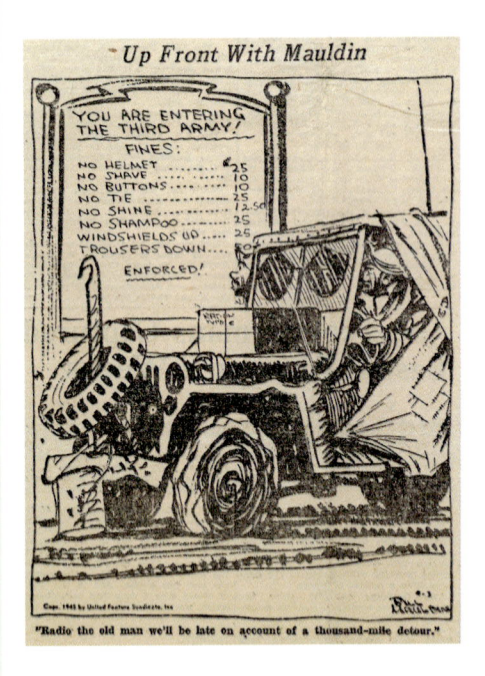

▶ Lower left and right: *"It's best not to speak to paratroopers about saluting. They always ask where you got your jump boots."* Original drawing and published appearance: drawing for a newspaper cartoon (black ink, black crayon, white correction paint, over pencil) published in *The Stars and Stripes* and other newspapers as the example shown right. Signed *Bill Mauldin* (lower left; hand signed in black ink), c. January 27, 1945. Copyright 1945 by Bill Mauldin. Courtesy of Bill Mauldin Estate LLC. Notes: The message of this cartoon would have been understood by many of the GIs on the front line, but its meaning would have been lost to the general public. Unlike most infantrymen, who were issued boots that had laces at the bottom and buckles at the top, paratroopers were given special boots that had simply high laces. These "jump boots" gave the paratrooper's ankles more support when landing on the ground after parachuting out of an aircraft. It was considered fashionable and prestigious for any soldier to wear jump boots, and therefore many of them were pilfered by officers in the infantry. The demand for jump boots was so great that there was a shortage of them; therefore, the paratroopers were often forced to wear standard-issue GI boots. In Mauldin's cartoon, the two officers are wearing jump boots while the unfortunate paratrooper is wearing standard-issue boots. —PMR

[original drawing]

[as published]

that the cartoons offered moments of needed relief to the men. Mauldin told an interviewer years later that "I always admired Patton. Oh, sure, the stupid bastard was crazy. He was insane. He thought he was living in the Dark Ages. Soldiers were peasants to him. I didn't like that attitude, but I certainly respected his theories and the techniques he used to get his men out of their foxholes." Despite Patton's negative attitude, many officers were convinced that the aim of Mauldin's cartoons was not to criticize authority but to present a documentation of true military life encased in a shell of comedy. "The only way I can try to be a little funny," Mauldin would later explain, "is to make something out of the humorous situations which come up even when you don't think life could be any more miserable."

Even with such criticisms, by March 1944, Mauldin was respected enough to be given his own Jeep to move about the front. This prized Jeep was, to Mauldin, a symbol of his artistic liberation, and with this freedom he roamed the war zone collecting material and producing six cartoons a week. The War Department, which had often been critical of Mauldin in the past, now realized the great influence of his work. Not only were the drawings offering an outlet for the common soldier, they were also helping to publicize the ground forces to the civilians back home. The government and the public increasingly adored Willie and Joe. Moreover, in recognition of his talent, after the Allied victory in Europe, on May 8, 1945, Bill Mauldin became the youngest person in history to win a Pulitzer Prize. His published book at the time, *Up Front*, was also selling so fast that demand could hardly be met. Bill's character Willie even made the cover of *Time Magazine* in the June 18, 1945 issue.

"They are so damned sick & tired of having their noses rubbed in a stinking war that their only ambition will be to forget it," Mauldin had once stated about all men returning home from the rigors of combat. Be that as it may, Bill Mauldin was now a household name, and fame seemed to be an awkward fit for the 23 year-old war veteran. In June 1945, Bill landed in La Guardia Field in New York and began a new chapter of his life. Even though Mauldin loved recognition, he seemed bothered by the hassles and restraints of stardom.

Post war, Willie and Joe became veterans making the difficult adjustment to domestic life back in the States. In these cartoons, his alienated combat infantrymen were transformed into clean-faced family men, struggling to adapt to the monotonous suburban culture. Feeling unable to continue their story successfully, however, Mauldin switched his interests to political cartooning, acting, freelance writing, and even made an unsuccessful run for Congress. Eventually, he stationed himself as an editorial cartoonist at the *St. Louis Post-Dispatch* and served there from 1958 until 1962.

It was in 1959 that Mauldin won his second Pulitzer Prize and the National Cartoonist Society Award for Editorial Cartooning. By 1962, he relocated to the *Chicago Sun-Times*, where he remained until, unfortunately, he was forced to retire. In 1991, while working on his beloved Jeep, his drawing hand was injured and rendered unusable. The same type of vehicle that allowed the artistic freedom of his military days, ultimately put an end to his career just weeks before his 70th birthday.

Regrettably, a few years later Bill began showing initial symptoms of Alzheimer's disease. As his mental faculties started to deteriorate, Mauldin's family reopened the stacks of fan mail that Bill had not read in decades. Those World War II veterans' letters were Bill's source of light in his last months. He did not always recall friends and family or remember the details of his marriages or career, but Mauldin never forgot the veterans, even in his most confused state. They were his bulwark. On January 22, 2003, three months after his 81st birthday, Bill Mauldin died.

[*Matthews' essay continues on page 41*]

▲ Drawing of an Army two star General (crayon), signed *B. Mauldin* (lower right; hand signed in black ink), c. 1945. Copyright 1945 by Bill Mauldin. Courtesy of Bill Mauldin Estate LLC. Notes: With this drawing, Mauldin is satirizing officers — especially General George Patton.

Patton expected his soldiers, enlisted men and officers alike, to be properly dressed at all times. (In one of his cartoons [page 36 top left], Mauldin illustrates that a strict dress code was enforced whenever a soldier entered the area of Patton's Third Army.)

In addition, Patton's soldiers were never allowed to have their hands in their pockets when they were standing. The drawing shows a two star general properly dressed, but overweight, smoking a cigarette, and sleeping on his feet. Furthermore, against Patton's strict rule, the general has his hands in his pockets. —PMR

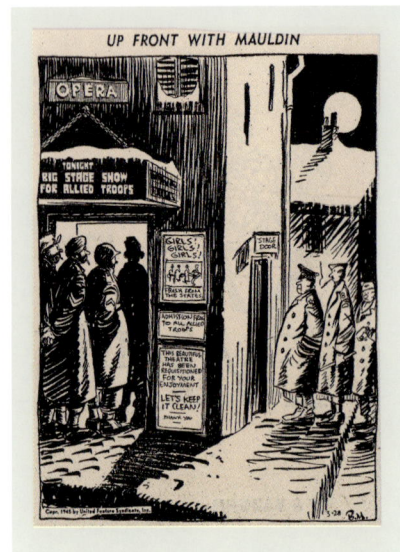

FLORIDA STATE UNIVERSITY INSTITUTE ON WORLD WAR II

▲ Printed cartoon without caption: *Up Front With Mauldin* (published in *The Journal*, Portland, Oregon), signed *B.M.* (lower right; signed in the plate), *c.* March 28, 1944 (previously published in *The Stars and Stripes*, Mediterranean edition, January 29, 1945). Copyright 1944 by Bill Mauldin. Courtesy of Bill Mauldin Estate LLC.

▶ "*My, sir- what an enthusiastic welcome!*" Newspaper with a printed cartoon: *Up Front with Mauldin* published in *The Stars and Stripes*, New York-Paris-London edition; Vol. 1, No. 103, signed *Bill Mauldin* (lower right; signed in the plate), Wednesday, November 1, 1944 (this cartoon was previously published in *The Stars and Stripes*, Mediterranean edition, September 16, 1944). Copyright 1944 by Bill Mauldin. Courtesy of Bill Mauldin Estate LLC.

▶ Facing page: Drawing of Joe (crayon), signed *Bill Mauldin* (lower right; hand signed in black ink; the complete inscribed text reads *To Fred with best regards / Bill Mauldin*), *c.* 1945. 'Willie' and 'Joe' characters, Copyright 1945 by Bill Mauldin. Courtesy of Bill Mauldin Estate LLC. Notes: With many of the posters that were produced by the government during World War II, the American soldier was depicted as a strong, well-groomed, ideal male specimen. Mauldin preferred to show the American GI in a more realistic manner —fatigued, sweaty and dirty, and with physical imperfections. His realistic approach illustrated the suffering many of the soldiers endured after an extended period of time fighting on the front lines.

[*continued in sidebar on page 39*]

SELECTIONS FROM THE COLLECTION OF DR. PATRICK M. ROWE

"The Battle of Mauldin"

Like many of the enlisted men during World War II, Bill Mauldin objected to the numerous perks enjoyed by officers. When soldiers were on transport ships, on leave from the front, looking for female companionship, or simply trying to obtain a drink of alcohol, the inequity between the enlisted men and officers was obvious to all the GIs. With many of his cartoons, Mauldin drew attention to this unjust situation.

There were some officers who supported Mauldin's criticisms. General Dwight Eisenhower (Supreme Allied Commander), General Oscar Solbert (Chief of Special Services in the European Theater), and other high ranking officers realized that Mauldin's satirical cartoons lifted the morale of the GIs and allowed their pent up frustrations to be released. Some officers even requested original drawings from Mauldin!

But, there were a number of officers who were highly critical of Mauldin's characterization of officers and thought that he was being insubordinate. Because Mauldin exposed the way these officers took advantage of their privileges of rank, they attempted to silence him. The most notable opponent of Mauldin's cartoons was General George "Old Blood and Guts" Patton, commander of the American Third Army.

Patton was so outraged by Mauldin's portrayal of American officers, as well as his representation of grimy GIs like Willie and Joe, he once threatened to stop the distribution of *The Stars and Stripes* within his area of command and stated that "if that little son of a bitch (Bill Mauldin) sets foot in the Third Army, I'll throw his ass in jail."

To relieve the troublesome situation between Sergeant Mauldin and General Patton, a meeting was arranged where the two men could talk privately and hopefully solve this problem that, if not worked out, could evolve into a publicity disaster that might damage the war effort. During the meeting, Patton pulled out of his desk drawer a number of Mauldin's cartoons that he considered to be disrespectful to the military. The two cartoons on page 38 were among this group.

◀ One of the cartoons shows an officer being pelted with fruit thrown by enlisted men in the transport behind and his driver. The other depicts enlisted men waiting at the front door of a theater where they can see girls perform in a USO show while officers stand at the back door waiting to actually meet the girls. Mauldin's get-together with Patton concluded with the high ranking General believing he had been triumphant over the lowly Sergeant. However, after the meeting Mauldin stated that "We parted good friends, but I don't think we changed each other's opinions." This outraged Patton and, once again, the General threatened to have Mauldin incarcerated. Finally, General Eisenhower came to Mauldin's rescue, proclaiming in a letter that Bill Mauldin was to be left alone. In his biography of Bill Mauldin, the historian Thomas DePastino describes how Captain Butcher, the officer who arranged the meeting between Mauldin and Patton, recorded that "It looks to me as if General Patton...has lost the battle of Mauldin."

During his career, Bill Mauldin was awarded the Pulitzer Prize twice. His first Pulitzer Prize, which he received in May, 1945 when he was only twenty-three years old, made him the youngest person in history to achieve this honor. Mauldin's first cartoon that the Pulitzer Prize committee judged to be the best of the year (on page 40) is included in the exhibition. This cartoon, with the caption *Fresh, spirited American troops, flushed with victory, are bringing in thousands of hungry, ragged, battle-weary prisoners*" (News item.), illustrates that, in fact, both the German and American soldiers were ragged and fatigued from battle. Since Mauldin did not believe that this was one of his best cartoons, he was somewhat shocked when he heard it was selected as the prize winner. Mauldin was awarded his second Pulitzer Prize for a cartoon he created in 1958 while working for the *St. Louis Post-Dispatch*.

—PMR

In his book *Up Front*, Mauldin attempted to describe what daily life was like for a soldier in combat:

Dig a hole in your backyard while it is raining. Sit in the hole until the water climbs up around your ankles. Pour cold mud down your shirt collar. Sit there for forty-eight hours, and, so there is no danger of your dozing off, imagine that a guy is sneaking around waiting for a chance to club you on the head or set your house on fire.

Get out of the hole, fill a suitcase full of rocks, pick it up, put a shotgun in your other hand, and walk on the muddiest road you can find. Fall flat on your face every few minutes as you imagine big meteors streaking down to sock you.

After ten or twelve miles (remember- you are still carrying the shotgun and suitcase) start sneaking through the wet brush. Imagine that somebody has booby-trapped your route with rattlesnakes which will bite you if you step on them. Give some friend a rifle and have him blast in your direction once in a while.

Snoop around until you find a bull. Try to figure out a way to sneak around him without letting him see you. When he does see you, run like hell all the way back to your hole in the back yard, drop the suitcase and shotgun, and get in.

If you repeat this performance every three days for several months, you may begin to understand why an infantryman sometimes gets out of breath. But you still won't understand how he feels when things get tough. —PMR

FLORIDA STATE UNIVERSITY INSTITUTE ON WORLD WAR II

▲ *"Fresh, spirited American troops, flushed with victory, are bringing in thousands of hungry, ragged, battle weary prisoners."* (News Item.) Printed Cartoon: *Up Front With Mauldin* (published in the *Daily News*, Los Angeles, California), not signed, Wednesday, November 8, 1944 (previously published in *The Stars and Stripes*, Mediterranean edition, October 13, 1944). Copyright 1944 by Bill Mauldin. Courtesy of Bill Mauldin Estate LLC.

▶ *"Joe, yestiddy ya saved me life an' I swore I'd pay ya back. Here's me last pair o' dry socks."* Printed cartoon: *Up Front...By Mauldin* published in *The Stars and Stripes*, Mediterranean edition, signed *Bill Mauldin* (lower left; signed in the plate), Thursday, March 2, 1944. Copyright 1944 by Bill Mauldin. Courtesy of Bill Mauldin Estate LLC. Notes: Often dry socks were crucial to the soldiers fighting for extended periods of time on the front lines. Wearing wet socks in winter could cause frost bite or trench foot, sometimes bringing about the need for amputation. A dry pair of socks could be as valuable as gold to an infantryman. —PMR

SELECTIONS FROM THE COLLECTION OF DR. PATRICK M. ROWE

[*Matthews' essay continued from page 37*]

While casting a light on the truth of combat, Bill Mauldin had kept alive a tradition of bold commentary that included the likes of Honoré Daumier, Mark Twain, Sinclair Lewis, and Charlie Chaplin. Mauldin's cartoons made him a hero to the common soldier. "They are rough and their language gets coarse because they live a life stripped of convention and niceties," Mauldin stated in his book *Up Front*.

> Their nobility and dignity come from the way they live unselfishly and risk their lives to help each other. They are normal people who have been put where they are, and whose actions and feelings have been molded by their circumstances…But when they are all together and they are fighting, despite their bitching and griping and goldbricking and mortal fear, they are facing cold steel and screaming lead and hard enemies, and they are advancing and beating the hell out of the opposition…They wish to hell they were someplace else, and they wish to hell they would get relief. They wish to hell the mud was dry and they wish to hell their coffee was hot. They want to go home. But they stay in their wet holes and fight, and then they climb out and crawl through minefields and fight some more.

An overwhelming number of gifts and letters arrived for Bill Mauldin upon his death. Many of the World War II soldiers claimed that his cartoons had kept their "humanity alive" and "saved countless souls from darkness." One veteran was interviewed saying, "You would have to be part of a combat infantry unit to appreciate what moments of relief Bill gave us. You had to be reading a soaking wet *Stars and Stripes* in a water-filled foxhole and then see one of his cartoons."

One such remembered cartoon of Mauldin's illustrated the two soldiers, Willie and Joe, huddled together in the reeds, their feet wet and buried in the mud, and a caption reading, "Joe, yestiddy ya saved me life an' I swore I'd pay ya back. Here's me last pair o' dry socks." Willie thanks his friend with his most precious possessions. What would seem like a minor thing to a civilian could have been a life saving gift to a fellow comrade during a time when trench foot and influenza were everyday realities. Upon Bill Mauldin's death, a single pair of dry, cotton socks was delivered to his family. This one gift moved Bill's son, David, to tears. That simple gift, like the words of Willie and Joe, seemed to speak for an entire nation of soldiers, thanking Sgt. Bill Mauldin for saving their lives during World War II, armed only with his pen, wit, and honesty.

Catherine Kendall Matthews, BA (Art History), graduated from University of West Florida in 2012. She was the Curatorial Intern for The Art Gallery (TAG) at UWF from 2011 until 2012. During this internship, her writings were presented in various exhibitions. For the past two years, she has been living in Paris, France, teaching English as a second language and working as a freelance writer and photographer documenting the solo female travel experience.

ACKNOWLEDGMENTS

Several people assisted with the production of the original catalogue for the exhibitions in Pensacola. The Mauldin Estate generously granted permission to publish the paintings, drawings, and prints in the catalogue. Jonathan Gordon and Alicia Lizarraga assisted in solving all the copyright issues. Mike Fleming, David Funk, Sara Smith, and Susi Turzanski-Wilbanks aided editing the text and Warren Thompson and Christopher White contributed photographic assistance. Finally, the faculty and staff at the University of West Florida Art Department and The Art Gallery (TAG) provided support that was crucial to the initial realization of this project. I would like to thank all of these friends for their encouragement and guidance. The TAG publication was dedicated to Maddie Loudon who turned four while work was in progress. Thanks to the Willies and Joes of World War II, Maddie lives in freedom today. —PMR

▲ *The Stars and Stripes* issue of December 9, 1942. Collection of Patrick M. Rowe.

▲ *"IT'S IKE HIMSELF. PASS THE WORD."* Printed cartoon, signed *Mauldin © 1969 Chicago Sun-Times* (lower right; signed in the plate); *Bill Mauldin* (lower left; hand signed in blue ink; the complete inscribed text reads *For Ed Pania with regards. Bill Mauldin*), 1969. Copyright 1969 by Bill Mauldin. Courtesy of Bill Mauldin Estate LLC.

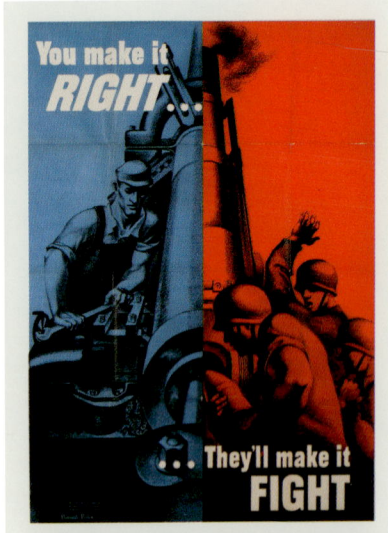

FLORIDA STATE UNIVERSITY INSTITUTE ON WORLD WAR II

▲ *You make it RIGHT... They'll make it FIGHT*, Bernard Perlin, 1942, United States War Production Board.

▲ *THIS IS THE ENEMY*, 1943. *Artist*: unknown.

▶ *UNITED we are strong / UNITED we will win*, Henry Koerner, 1943, United States Government Printing Office.

▶ Facing page: United States Hospital Ship Flag, 1944-1945. *Inscription*: USA.T. JOHN L. CLEM. (stamped against the field of the flag). From 1941 until 1943, the John L. Clem served as a United States Army transport ship. In 1944, at the shipyard in Mobile, Alabama, the army converted her into a hospital ship. Subsequently, from 1944 until 1945, she served in the western Mediterranean.

SELECTIONS FROM THE COLLECTION OF DR. PATRICK M. ROWE

THE DESIGN OF WAR
WORLD WAR WII PROPAGANDA POSTERS AND FLAGS

Selections from the Collection of Dr. Patrick M. Rowe

Christina Glover

World War II was the most significant and catastrophic event of the twentieth century. To commemorate the soldiers who took part in the war, the Florida State University Museum of Fine Arts presents *The Design of War*, original World War II posters and flags on loan from the collection of Dr. Patrick Rowe, art history professor at Pensacola State College and collector of nineteenth- and twentieth-century prints. The flags and propaganda posters demonstrate how visual media communicated messages that supported the war effort and led to victory for the Allies. The posters illustrate themes such as recruiting, fundraising drives, conservation of resources, defense, victory, and the preservation of freedom. They document the messages that the government and private industry presented to both the American public and the troops, and they provide the contemporary viewer with an understanding of the crucial role art played as part of the war effort. The flags on display form an important and educational component of the exhibition. To the citizens and soldiers taking part in the war, the design of a flag communicated a message and commonly evoked an emotional patriotic feeling. However, during peacetime, the symbolism of these flags and the deep sense of patriotism they created are often forgotten. With this exhibition, the significance of these flags to those who personally experienced the wars is made clear for the viewer.

The Golden Age of posters began in the late-nineteenth century and continued until the mid-twentieth century. Master artists like Henri de Toulouse-Lautrec, Jules Chéret, and Alphonse Mucha raised this medium to the level of fine art. Many of the works in the exhibition are created in the traditional poster technique of color lithography. Other posters are made using a photomechanical process, a state-of-the-art printing technique during World War II. The posters parallel contemporary styles in painting, and they are as much a part of the visual culture as their painted counterparts. Posters in the exhibition reflect the stylistic features of Art Deco, Expressionism, Social Realism, and other art movements.

Posters were used as a form of communication because they were inexpensive to produce, they were easily accessible to the public, and they effectively conveyed a message. Their purpose was to visually persuade the audience–often to mobilize them into action (to enlist, to save resources, to work in an artillery factory, or to buy war bonds). Regardless of the theme, the posters were propaganda, which has been a function of visual media since its earliest history.

The design of most war posters made in the United States depended on a direct connection between text and image. Patriotism was a driving force, as was fear of the enemy. The poster *You make it RIGHT... They'll make it FIGHT* created a link between the product in the factory and the weapon in the field. Images and text appear in red, white, and blue, almost as a detail of the American flag itself. The composition is divided in half; both sides (the home front and the front line) are presumably equal contributors to the war effort. As with many posters related to

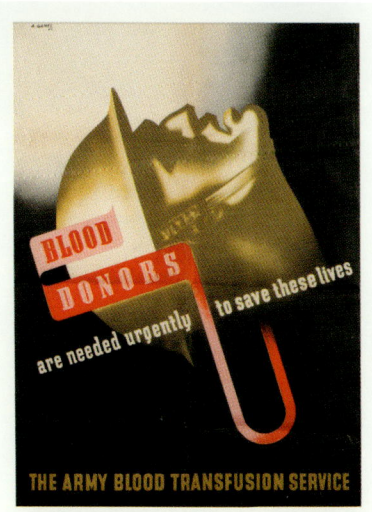

▲ *BLOOD DONORS are needed urgently to save these lives / THE ARMY BLOOD TRANSFUSION SERVICE*, Abram Games, c. 1942, published by Her Majesty's Stationary Service for the Army Transfusion Service, printed by W. R. Royal and Son, Ltd., London.

Because of his poster designs, Abram Games is recognized as one of the greatest graphic artists of the twentieth century. Describing the propaganda impact of his graphic designs, Games stated, "I wind the spring and the public, in looking at the poster, will have that spring released in its mind."

43

▲United States Service Flag, 1942-1945. *Inscription*: THE NAME ANNIN GUARANTEES QUALITY / DEFIANCE / REG. US PAT. OFF. / TWO PLY-MOTH PROOF / GUARANTEED DEFIANCE FAST COLORS / 3x5 ft. (stamped along the hoist). Reportedly, this service flag was on display in a church during World War II. It is decorated with 98 blue stars (70 on the front and 28 on the back), four gold stars (on the front), and two red stars (one on the front and one on the back).

▲United States Service Flag, 1942-1945. *Inscription*: none. Set against the field of this flag are two appliquéd blue stars and a red cross. The red cross indicates that a member of the family is serving as a doctor, nurse, medic, or corpsman.

▶*BUY WAR BONDS*, attributed to N.C. Wyeth, 1942, United States Government Printing Office.

SELECTIONS FROM THE COLLECTION OF DR. PATRICK M. ROWE

the theme of war production, it is dramatically suggested that the work of a single individual in a factory will determine the nation's victory or defeat in war.

Sometimes the subject of the posters consisted of only text that related a message in a direct, clear manner. Other times the subject was simply a depiction of an idealized, heroic soldier or factory worker and a short line of text relating a message that, at a glance, most Americans could easily understand. However, occasionally the patrons commissioning posters relied on the expert eye of talented artists and commercial illustrators to create bold and dramatic designs. For example, Abram Games' poster *BLOOD DONORS are needed urgently to save these lives* is a masterpiece in design. His composition, color, text, and images are powerfully arranged to fully awaken the emotions of the public. Because of the originality of his compositions, today Games is recognized as one of the greatest graphic artists of the twentieth century. Some artists and illustrators had reputations that were established prior to the war. The most notable example was Norman Rockwell, a celebrated artist who contributed his work at no cost to the war effort. In 1942, Rockwell created his widely known series of paintings–the *Four Freedoms* (see page 54).

The *Four Freedoms* paintings, which were based on a speech given by Franklin D. Roosevelt in 1941, were transposed into four posters. The paintings were sent to sixteen cities around the United States and raised 133 million dollars to support the war effort. Rockwell's posters were used to encourage people to buy bonds for war production, and by the end of World War II, four million had been printed by the government. His work *Freedom from Want* emphasizes family and national values, as well as religious gratitude. It portrays an image (Thanksgiving Day dinner) with which most Americans could identify and relates a cause (national prosperity) for which all would be willing to fight.

Complementing the posters are original World War II flags, some of which are shown in the posters themselves. A number of these are United States Navy signal flags that indicated words and letters to other passing American vessels. As with traditional art forms, the flags served as visual cues to language. Other flags in the exhibition are United States service flags, also known as "son in service flags." These were displayed in homes and towns, with a star representing each soldier who was either serving in the war (a blue star) or who had died in war (a gold star). The poster *...because somebody talked!* shows the service flag of a deceased solider to make a strong but sentimental appeal to the viewer. A teary-eyed spaniel mourns the loss of his owner, due only to someone's careless talk, and implicitly asks Americans to maintain secrecy about war-related information.

By bringing together a collection of World War II posters and flags, this exhibition is meant to honor the men and women of "The Greatest Generation" who fought for American national values and against the evils of totalitarianism. In addition to the collection's visual and historical appeal, it brings awareness to the present-day issues facing our most recent veterans from the wars in Iraq and Afghanistan. Just as the posters from World War II called attention to the troubles facing the troops, this exhibition reminds us of our job at home to support those who are fighting for us abroad.

Christina Glover, MA (Art History), graduated from Florida State University in 2012. She is currently teaching at Pensacola State College in Pensacola, Florida, where she specializes in American and German Modernism, with a particular interest in the Bauhaus and its legacy.

ACKNOWLEDGMENTS

I wish to thank the director, curator, and staff at the Pensacola Museum of Art for their assistance in developing the exhibition The Design of War. This exhibition, which included both World War I and World War II objects, was on display at the PMA from November 2013 through January 2014. —PMR

▲ *...because somebody talked!*, Wesley, 1944, United States Government Printing Office.

▲ *A careless word... ...A NEEDLESS SINKING.* 1942. Artist: Anton Otto Fischer.

45

FLORIDA STATE UNIVERSITY INSTITUTE ON WORLD WAR II

▲United State Under Secretary of the Navy Flag, March, 1943. *Inscription*: UNDER SECRETARY OF NAVY / NO 4 / MARE ISLAND / MAR 1943 (stamped along the hoist). When this flag was produced, in March of 1943, James Forrestal was serving as the Under Secretary of the Navy. From 1944 until 1945, Forrestal was appointed Secretary of the Navy, the highest-ranking civilian in that branch of the military.

▲*An adequate NATIONAL DEFENSE is our greatest assurance of PEACE / America needs A NAVY SECOND TO NONE!* c. 1940. *Artist*: unknown.

SELECTIONS FROM THE COLLECTION OF DR. PATRICK M. ROWE

Notes from the DESIGN OF WAR Collection

Patrick M. Rowe, PhD

◀ United States Army M1 Helmet, 1944. A vital piece of protective equipment used by infantrymen during both world wars was the steel helmet. Numerous companies in the United States produced the M-1917 brimmed helmets used by the American soldiers during World War I. Their design was based on the British Mark 1 helmet first produced in 1916. It consisted of an interior cloth liner that was permanently attached by rivets to the lip of the exterior steel shell. Various nicknames were used by the Americans and British to refer to these helmets. Since the earliest version was developed by the Englishman John Leopold Brodie, the British most commonly called it simply the "Brodie helmet." Americans often referred to it as the "doughboy helmet."

In 1941, the United States replaced the World War I style M-1917 helmet with the more streamlined M1 helmet. During the course of World War II, over 22 million of these helmets were produced. The M1 helmet consisted of two parts, a plastic and cloth liner and a manganese steel shell, that could be easily separated. The specimen on display in the exhibition has a shell that was made in 1944. The liner was manufactured by the Westinghouse Company sometime between 1941 and 1945. During the 1950s, probably during the Korean War, decals and a new sweat-band were added to the liner, and, subsequently, it was repainted in dark olive green.

◀ United States Military Garrison Cap, 1942. *Inscription*: CAPS, GARRISON COTTON KHAKI / Size 7 ½ / SARPELY CAP CO. / Cont. W-869-QM-20353 / DATED JULY 28, 1942 / Spec. No. 8-114-B Type II / DATED JUNE 2, 1942 / STOCK No. 73-C-18012 / Phila. Q.M. Depot (stamped on a label sewed onto the interior liner). United States soldiers first began to wear cloth garrison caps during World War I. They were designed with straight sides and a center that is indented from front to back. Often an emblem signifying the soldier's rank was pinned to the front on the left side. Because of their unpopularity with the soldiers and their grooved shape, the GIs commonly used derogatory sexual nick-names to refer to them.

◀ United States Army Identification Tags, 1944. *Inscription*: Obverse: ROWE, THOMAS H / 13153692 T 44 A / C. Attached to the identification tag chain is a St. Christopher's metal that was given to Private Rowe by his fiancée, Dorothy Johnson. In 1906, the requirement of wearing military identification tags (colloquially referred to as "dog tags") was officially authorized by the United States War Department. This policy was initiated for a gruesome, practical reason: if a soldier's body had been mutilated beyond recognition during combat, often the only means of identification was by this tag. Initially, each soldier was issued a single tag. However, in 1916, it was decided that every soldier should wear two identification tags. With this system, if a soldier died, one tag would be left with the body for identification while the other would be removed and given to the military authorities who were in charge of recording the death. In 1918, to make the recording process more efficient, serial numbers were also stamped onto the identification tags. During World War I, identification tags were simply circular metal disks strung together with a cloth cord that would have been worn around the neck.

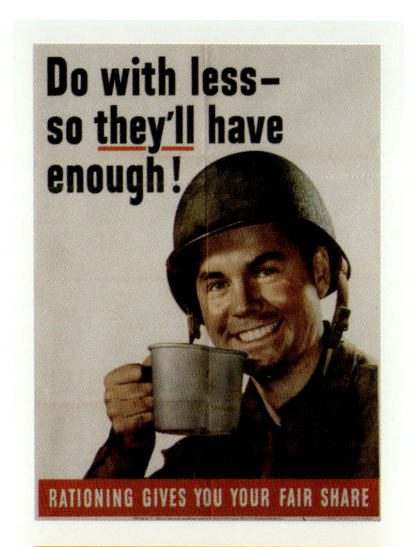

▲ *Do with less – so they'll have enough! / RATIONING GIVES YOU YOUR FAIR SHARE*, 1943. *Artist*: unknown.

▲ *THIS MEANS X OUT OF BOUNDS (OFF-LIMITS) TO ALL ALLIED TROOPS*, c. 1944-45. *Artist*: unknown.

■ The artifacts and historic photographs of of Patrick M. Rowe have been photographed by Christopher White, Pensacola, Florida.

FLORIDA STATE UNIVERSITY INSTITUTE ON WORLD WAR II

▲ United Kingdom Royal Navy White Ensign, 1944.

▲ United State Navy Union Jack, 1944.

▶ *UNITED / THE UNITED NATIONS FIGHT FOR FREEDOM.* 1943. *Artist*: Leslie Darrell Ragan.

SELECTIONS FROM THE COLLECTION OF DR. PATRICK M. ROWE

Normally, the soldier's name, rank, company, military branch, and country are listed on the obverse, and his serial number is listed on the reverse.

Unlike the identification tags from World War I, where information was hand engraved onto metal circular discs, the information on the tags from World War II was mechanically stamped onto metal oblong plates with rounded corners. In addition, a metal chain was used to wear the tags around the neck rather than a cloth strap. Medical information such as blood type of the soldier was recorded, and the religious preference could also be stamped onto the tag: variations evolved from P for Protestant, C for Catholic, and H for Jewish (from the word Hebrew). In the European Theater, for captured soldiers who were Jewish, the stamping of religion could have consequences.

◀ United Kingdom Royal Navy White Ensign, November, 1944. *Inscription*: (admiralty stamp) / 6 / WHITE ENS. / J.W. PLANT & Co. LTD. / RICHMOND FACTORY / 9 ELSIE CRESCENT. LEEDS 1. / NOV 1944 (stamped along the hoist). During World War II, the White Ensign was hoisted on British military ships bearing the prefix HMS (His Majesty's Ship) and was flown at all naval shore establishments. Since the date November, 1944, is stamped along the hoist of this flag, its production can be securely dated to World War II.

◀ United States Navy Union Jack, 1944. *Inscription*: UNION JACK / No. 6 / MI 44 (stamped along the hoist). The United States Navy Union Jack is a military flag that was flown from the vertical staff (the jackstaff) at the bow of the ship. During World War II, its design consisted simply of the canton (the blue rectangle with white stars) of the United States Navy Ensign. Normally, the Union Jack was raised when the ship was docked at port, and as soon as the ship left the dock it was taken down. The Union Jack was also flown when the ship was anchored at sea or dressed for a special occasion.

▼ *EVERY FIRE IS SABOTAGE TODAY! Artist*: Victor Keppler.

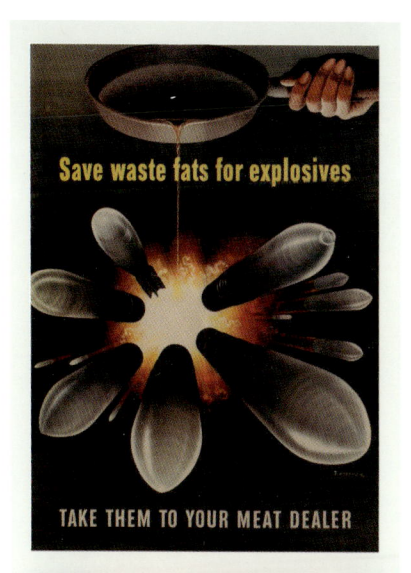

▲ *Save waste fats for explosives / TAKE THEM TO THE MEAT DEALER*. 1943. *Artist*: Henry Koerner. Because of the dramatic increase in manufacturing during World War II, there were shortages of many materials. Two of those materials were oils and butter (fats). Fats were needed to produce the vital substance glycerin, an ingredient used in the production of explosives. To alleviate this shortage, housewives were asked to save grease when cooking and turn over all fats to their local butcher or grocer, who then passed it on to the government for use in military industrial production.

▲ *Where our men are fighting / OUR FOOD IS FIGHTING / BUY WISELY — COOK CAREFULLY–STORE CAREFULLY–USE LEFTOVERS*. 1943. *Artist*: unknown.

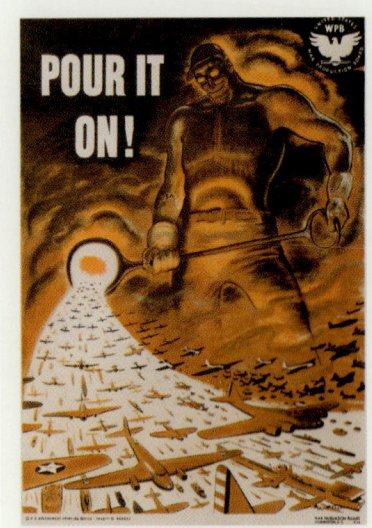

FLORIDA STATE UNIVERSITY INSTITUTE ON WORLD WAR II

▲ POUR IT ON! 1942. *Artist:* Garrett Price.

▲ *Kinda give it your personal attention, will you?* / *MORE PRODUCTION*. 1942. *Artist:* Herbert Roese.

▶ *The more WOMEN at work the sooner we WIN!* 1943. *Artist:* unknown.

50

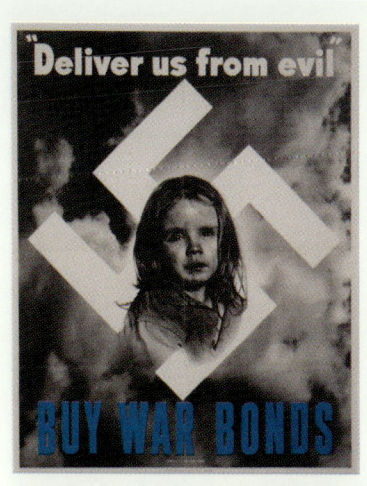

SELECTIONS FROM THE COLLECTION OF DR. PATRICK M. ROWE

▲ *"Deliver us from evil"* / BUY WAR BONDS. 1943. Artist: Harriet Nadeau.

▲ HITLER WANTS US TO BELIEVE THAT: Democracy is dying… / AMERICANS WILL NOT BE FOOLED! 1942. Artist: unknown.

◄ WHAT TO DO IN CASE OF AIR RAIDS, c. 1942. Artist: unknown.

51

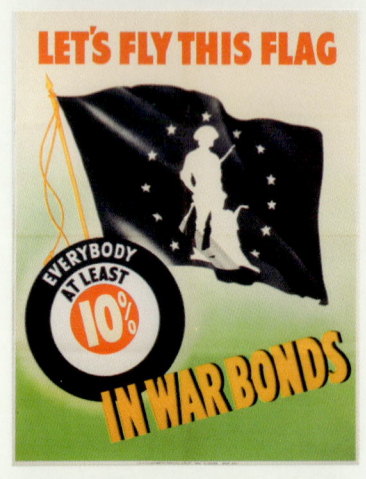

FLORIDA STATE UNIVERSITY INSTITUTE ON WORLD WAR II

▲ United States Department of the Treasury Minuteman Flag, 1942-1945. *Inscription*: none.

▲ *LET'S FLY THIS FLAG / EVERYBODY AT LEAST 10% IN WAR BONDS*. 1942.

SELECTIONS FROM THE COLLECTION OF DR. PATRICK M. ROWE

▲ *WE CAN... WE WILL.. WE MUST!.. Franklin D. Roosevelt / BUY U.S. WAR SAVING BONDS & STAMPS NOW*, 1942. *Artist*: Carl Paulson. This was the most replicated poster design in the United States during World War II. In addition to billboards showing the design being erected all across the country, over four million of these small posters were produced

◀ *LET'S FLY THIS FLAG / EVERYBODY AT LEAST 10% IN WAR BONDS*. 1942. *Artist*: unknown. To support the war effort, all 139 million Americans were encouraged to invest 10% of their income in war bonds. If an adequate number of employees purchased bonds, the company where they worked was allowed to fly the "Minuteman Flag" issued by the United States Department of the Treasury. This flag depicted the white silhouette of a Revolutionary War minuteman holding a musket and with a plow at his feet. These images were set against a patriotic blue background and surrounded by stars representing the thirteen colonies.

◀ *SOMETHING FOR THE BOYS / G.I. BONDS*, 1944. *Artist*: Alberto Vargas.

▼ World War II United States Savings Bond, December 7, 1944. This $100.00 war bond, which has never been redeemed, was bought by Mr. Solomon Mindell, a Jewish resident of Pensacola, Florida. It was issued on December 7, 1944 (now known as Pearl Harbor Day), at the Naval Aviation Station, Pensacola, Florida.

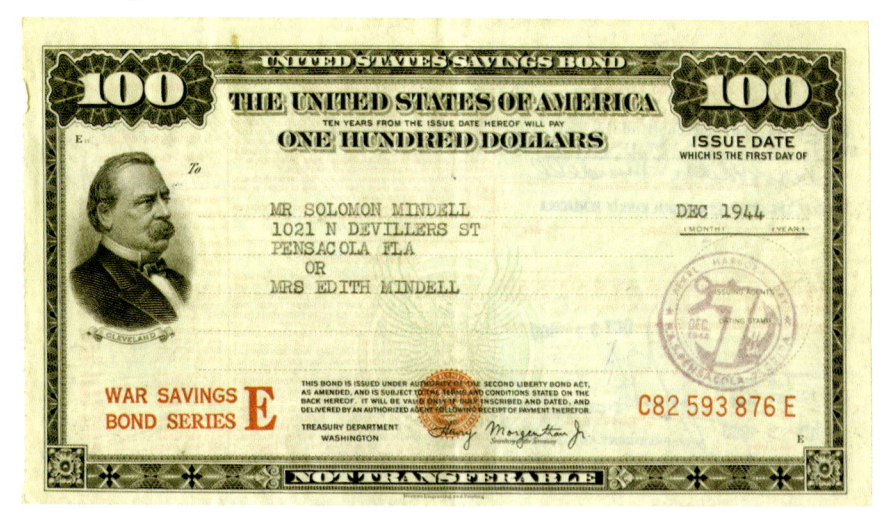

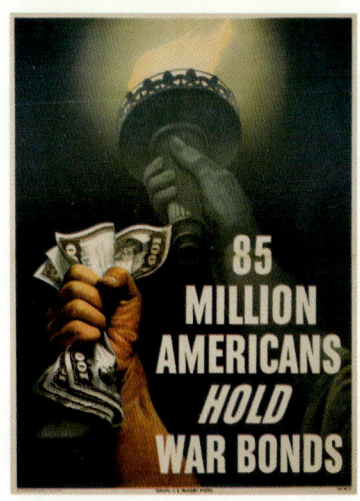

▲ United States Defense Savings Bond 10¢ Stamp, 1942-1945.

▲ *85 MILLION AMERICANS HOLD WAR BONDS*, 1945. *Artist*: unknown.

53

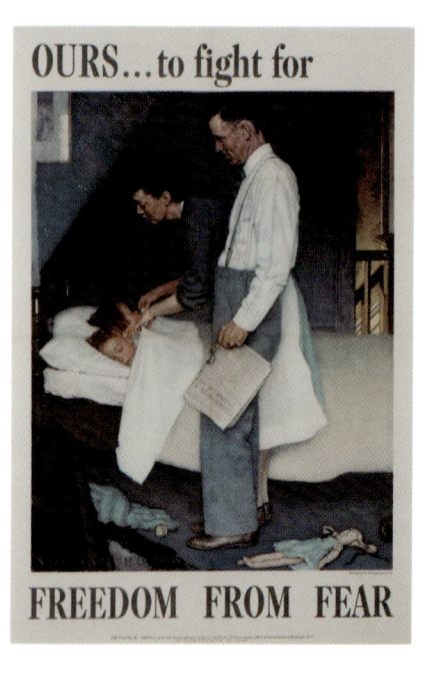

FLORIDA STATE UNIVERSITY INSTITUTE ON WORLD WAR II

Excerpt from President Franklin Delano Roosevelt's Annual Message to Congress on the State of the Union, January 6, 1941:

"In the future days, which we seek to make secure, we look forward to a world founded upon four essential human freedoms.

The first is freedom of speech and expression — everywhere in the world.

The second is freedom of every person to worship God in his own way — everywhere in the world.

The third is freedom from want — which, translated into world terms, means economic understandings which will secure to every nation a healthy peacetime life for its inhabitants- everywhere in the world.

The fourth is freedom from fear — which, translated into world terms, means a world-wide reduction of armaments to such a point and in such a thorough fashion that no nation will be in a position to commit an act of physical aggression against any neighbor — anywhere in the world."

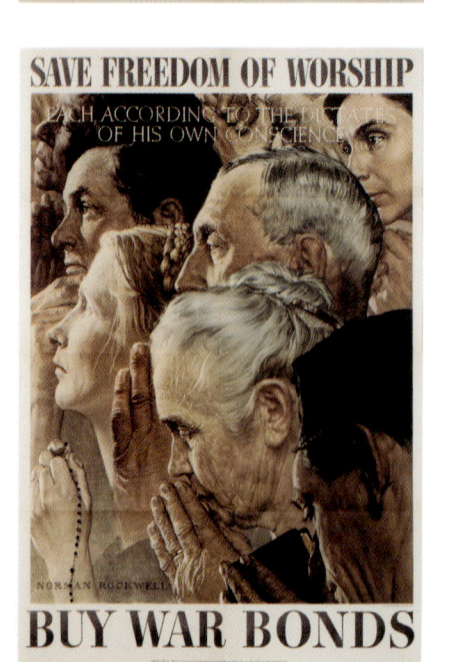

SELECTIONS FROM THE COLLECTION OF DR. PATRICK M. ROWE

◀ United States Service Flag, 1942-1945. *Inscription*: B. PASQUALE Co / MAKERS OF FLAGS & BANNERS (stamped on a tag along the back of the hoist). Flags of this type (sometimes referred to as "son in service flags") would have been displayed in the windows or hung from the porches of homes in the United States during both World War I and World War II. The number of blue stars on the flag signified how many family members were actively serving in the military. Gold stars indicated the number of family members enlisted in the military who had died and red stars represented captured or missing in action. Some of the service flags displayed silver stars. What these stars indicated is not clear. Most sources record they signified that family members fighting in the war had been disabled and, therefore, could no longer serve. Some service flags were hoisted in town halls and factories rather than homes. These flags, which usually were more substantial in size and often included numerous blue and gold stars, indicated how many citizens or workers were serving in the military or had died in the war.

◀ *Ours…to fight for / FREEDOM FROM WANT*. 1943. *Artist*: Norman Rockwell. In order to finance military operations and constrain inflation during World War II, the United States government sold defense bonds. Popular musicians, Hollywood stars, and famous artists used their talents to encourage citizens to "Buy Bonds." During the war, Norman Rockwell, one of the most renowned artists of that era, created a series of paintings to promote this cause.

The most successful of his paintings were the *Four Freedoms*. The inspiration for these paintings was Franklin D. Roosevelt's State of the Union address on January 6, 1941. In his speech, Roosevelt articulated the four basic freedoms that people of all countries should have the right to enjoy: freedom of speech, freedom of worship, freedom from want, and freedom from fear. These are the subjects illustrated by Rockwell.

After the completion of the paintings, they were sent on an exhibition tour around the country, raising over 132 million dollars for the war effort. They were also reproduced in *The Saturday Evening Post* and subsequently transposed into different size posters that were distributed to citizens all across the nation. Because of their wide spread popularity, by the end of World War II over 4 million of the posters had been produced by the government.

◀ *Ours…to fight for / FREEDOM FROM FEAR*. 1943. *Artist*: Norman Rockwell.

◀ *SAVE FREEDOM OF WORSHIP / BUY WAR BONDS*. 1943. *Artist*: Norman Rockwell.

◀ *SAVE FREEDOM OF SPEECH / BUY WAR BONDS*. 1943. *Artist*: Norman Rockwell.

▶ United States Service Flag, 1942-1945. *Inscription*: MEMBERS OF ST. MICHAELS SOCIETY / SERVED OUR COUNTRY (The letters are appliquéd against the front field of the flag). One gold star and 54 blues stars (39 on the front and 15 on the back) are in the fields of this flag. In addition, the numbers 105 and 1 are shown in the front field. What these numbers signify is not clear.

▶ United States Service Flag, 1942-1945. *Inscription*: none. This service flag is decorated with 19 blue stars, each one embroidered with the name of an American soldier. The fact that the same last names often appear on different stars — 4 Woods, 4 Halls, and 3 Crippins — reveals how common it was for several members from the same family to be serving in the military during World War II. The flag illustrates the degree to which families were willing to sacrifice for the war effort and how unified the country was in the fight against totalitarianism.

◀▲United States Service Flags, 1942-1945.

55

FLORIDA STATE UNIVERSITY INSTITUTE ON WORLD WAR II

▲ United States Navy Funeral Flag, February, 1944. *Inscription*: US ENSIGN NO 7 FUNERAL / MARE ISLAND / FEB 1944 (stamped along the hoist [i.e., the border of the flag nearest to the flagpole]).

▲ United States Service Flag, 1942-1945. Inscription: none. The stars on this flag indicate that, as was the case with the Sullivan brothers, five members from the family were serving in the military during the war.

▶ *The five Sullivan brothers "missing in action" off the Solomons / THEY DID THEIR PART.* 1943. *Artist*: unknown. On January 3, 1942, the Sullivan Brothers joined the

the five Sullivan brothers "missing in action" off the Solomons

THEY DID THEIR PART

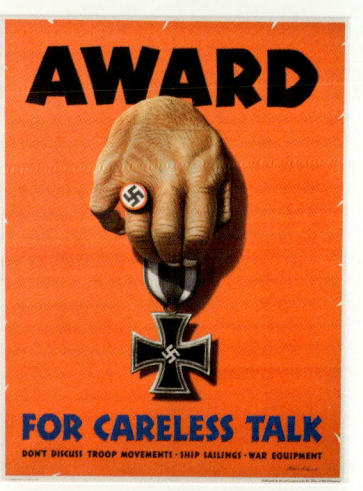

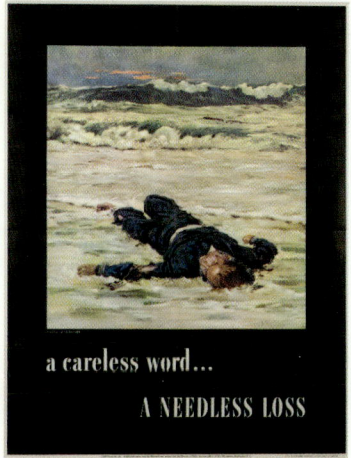

SELECTIONS FROM THE COLLECTION OF DR. PATRICK M. ROWE

United States Navy with the agreement that all five siblings would serve together.
[*continued in sidebar page 57*]
Although there was a military policy stipulating that siblings were to be separated while in the service, this rule was ignored. Tragically, all five of the brothers, George, Francis, Joseph, Madison, and Albert, died on the light cruiser *USS Juneau* when it was sunk in the South Pacific on November 13, 1942.

▲ AWARD FOR CARELESS TALK / DON'T DISCUSS TROOP MOVEMENTS SHIP SAILINGS • WAR EQUIPMENT. 1944. *Artist*: Stevan Dohanos.

▲ *A careless word...A NEEDLESS LOSS.* 1943. *Artist*: Anton Otto Fischer.

◀ *THIS IS A V HOME.* c. 1942. *Artist*: unknown.

57

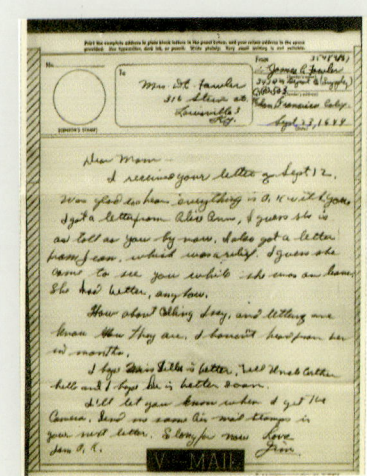

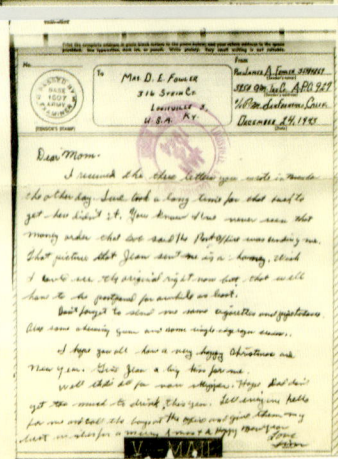

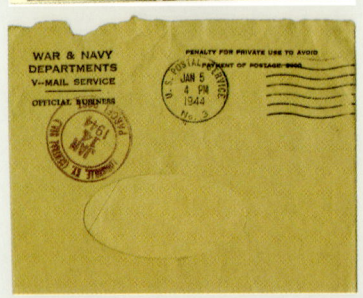

FLORIDA STATE UNIVERSITY INSTITUTE ON WORLD WAR II

▲ Letters written by James Arthur Fowler, Private, United States Army, from the collection of J. Scott Fowler, James Arthur Fowler's grandson. James Arthur Fowler was born in Louisville, Kentucky. He joined the United States Army in 1942 and served in Pacific Theater, both New Guinea and the Philippines. In 1945, he returned home where he was honorably discharged.

▶ *He's Sure to get V⋯–MAIL*, 1943. *Artist*: Schlaikjer.

SELECTIONS FROM THE COLLECTION OF DR. PATRICK M. ROWE

Thomas H. Rowe was born in Bethlehem, Pennsylvania. He joined the United States Army in 1944 and, during World War II, he flew in C47s and B24s over France, Belgium, and Germany. In 1945, he returned home where he was honorably discharged. Today, Thomas H. Rowe is 91 years old and lives in Gulf Stream, Florida. His letters in the collection were written to his fiancée, Dorothy M. Johnson.

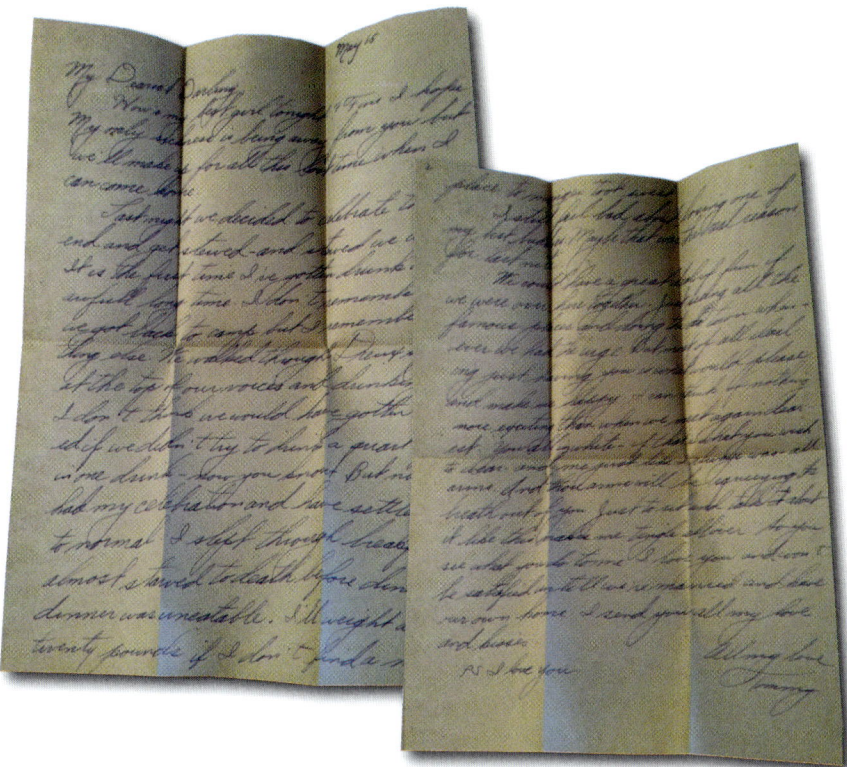

Letter written by Thomas H. Rowe, Staff Sergeant, United States Army Air Force from the Collection of Patrick M. Rowe, Thomas H. Rowe's son.

Spelling has been regularized in the transcription.

Feb 17 1945

My Sweetest Darling,

How are you today honey? Fine I hope.

There's been no mail for quite a spell. Can't understand it. But I guess one of these days he'll be presenting me with a bag full of letters and boxes.

Spring has set in and it's a relief to be rid of the cold winter weather. It's just perfect for walks in the country.

As for news, well there just isn't any. Life is dull and fast becoming routine.

At last my table has become complete. My writing still hasn't improved I'm afraid. Guess I'm just a scribbler at heart.

We've got a speaker hooked up to a neighbor's radio and it sure livens up the tent. Tonight we heard Abbot and Costello in their usual run of corn and enjoyed it very much. Now we're waiting for the hit parade. We get them a few weeks behind I believe. Last week we still had the, "Trolley Song," first.

The birthday present that Ruthie and Suzie sent me are on my table. The bottles are cute and the cologne smells good. Everybody envies them. And this is some of Aunt Laura's stationery I'm writing on.

You know honey there's something I'm hungry for that you can't get over here for love nor money. And that's mayonnaise. So if you could manage to acquire a large jar of white mayonnaise I sure would appreciate it. Could you hun; huh, please.

Nothing more that I have a yen for at present except you darling. But then I always have a desire for you. Cause I love you and find it hard to have to be so far from where my mind is. No matter where I go my thoughts are of you dearest. All my dreams are for us not just me. They include only two people honey, you and me. I send you all my love. I will always love you darling forever and ever.

All my love

Tommy

PS I love you

59

FLORIDA STATE UNIVERSITY INSTITUTE ON WORLD WAR II

German Radio Reports:

HITLER DEAD

THE STARS AND STRIPES
Paris Edition — Daily Newspaper of U.S. Armed Forces in the European Theater of Operations
Vol. 1—No. 279 — 1 Fr. — 1 Fr. — Wednesday, May 2, 1945
EXTRA — EXTRA

The German radio announced last night that Adolf Hitler had died yesterday afternoon, and that Adm. Doenitz, former commander-in-chief of the German Navy, had succeeded him as ruler of the Reich.

Doenitz, speaking later over the German radio, Reuter said, declared that "Hitler has fallen at his command post."

"My first task," Doenitz said, "is to save the German people from destruction by Bolshevism. If only for this task, the struggle will continue."

The announcement preceding the proclamation by Doenitz said: "It is reported from the Fuehrer's headquarters that our Fuehrer, Adolf Hitler, has fallen this afternoon at his command post in the Reich Chancellery, fighting to the last breath against Bolshevism and for his country. On April 30, the Fuehrer appointed Grand Adm. Doenitz as his successor. The new Fuehrer will speak to the German people."

The talk by Doenitz then followed, Reuter said. Doenitz said: "German men and women, soldiers of the German Wehrmacht, our Fuehrer, Adolf Hitler, has fallen. German people are in deepest mourning and veneration."

"Adolf Hitler recognized beforehand the terrible danger of Bolshevism," Doenitz said, "and devoted his life to fighting it. At the end of this, his battle, and of his unswerving straight path of life, stands his death as a hero in the capital of the Reich."

"All his life meant service to the German people. His battle against the Bolshevik flood benefited not only Europe but the whole world. The Fuehrer has
(Continued on Page 8)

Churchill Hints Peace Is at Hand

Winston Churchill indicated in a brief address to Commons yesterday that peace in Europe might come before Saturday.

Although he declined to give any statement on the reported surrender negotiations, the Prime Minister acknowledged that an important announcement was possible before the House adjourned Friday night. The admission was regarded as confirmation that the negotiations are well under way.

In Stockholm, meanwhile, Count Folke Bernadotte, head of the Swedish Red Cross gave virtual denial at a press conference that he was acting as go-between in peace negotiations between the Allies and the German government.

"I have not been Himmler during my last visit to Germany and Denmark, and I have not forwarded any message from Himmler or
(Continued on Page 8)

Pope Prepares Speech

ROME, May 1 (UP).—Reliable Vatican quarters said today that the Papal apartment has been prepared for an imminent worldwide broadcast by the Pope. The subject of the address is expected to be in connection with the end of the European war.

60

SELECTIONS FROM THE COLLECTION OF DR. PATRICK M. ROWE

◀ Rayon Nightgown and parachute, 1944. This is the nightgown made from the cloth from SSgt Thomas H. Rowe's World War II parachute. In the background is a remnant of a United States Army Air Force Parachute. This parachute was used by Staff Sergeant Thomas H. Rowe while flying missions over occupied France, Belgium, and Germany during World War II. After being honorably discharged from the military, SSgt Rowe retained his parachute and gave it to his mother who used the cloth to make a nightgown for his fiancée, Dorothy M. Johnson. Because of the shortage of quality fabric during and after the war, it was a common practice by many of the soldiers who served in the Army Air Force to reuse parachute cloth to make both nightgowns and wedding dresses for their brides-to-be.

May 15 [1945; 7 days after VE-Day]

My Dearest Darling,

How's my best girl tonight? Fine I hope. My only sickness is being away from you but we'll make up for all this lost time when I can come home.

Last night we decided to celebrate the war's end and get stewed-and-stewed we were. It is the first time I've gotten drunk in an awful long time. I don't remember how we got back to camp but I remember everything else. We walked through Dreux singing at the top our voices and drinking wine. I don't think we would have gotten so soused if we didn't try to drink a quart of wine in one drink — now you know. But now I've had my celebration and have settled down to normal. I slept through breakfast and almost starved to death before dinner. And dinner was uneatable. I'll weigh about twenty pounds if I don't find a new place to manger toot sweet.

I still feel bad about losing one my best buddies. Maybe that was the real reason for last nite.

We could have a great deal of fun if we were over here together. Just seeing all the famous places and doing the town whenever we had the urge. But most of all darling just having you is what would please and make me happy. I can think of nothing more exciting than when we meet again dearest. You all in white — if that's what you wish to wear — and me just like I always was — all arms. And those arms will be squeezing the breath out of you. Just to sit and talk about it like this makes me tingle all over. So you see what you do to me. I love you and won't be satisfied until we're married and have our own home. I send you all my love and kisses.

PS I love you

All my love

Tommy

Patrick M. Rowe graduated with his PhD in Art History from Florida State University in 1989. His area of research at that time was on Etruscan and Roman art and archaeology. From 1976 to 2002, he spent summers in Italy excavating at the Etrusco-Roman site of Cetamura. Since 1983, during the academic year he has taught art history at Pensacola State College, and from 1990 until 2010 he was a guest professor teaching in the Art Department at the University of West Florida. In 1998, he began taking a keen interest in eighteenth and early twentieth-century printmaking. Dr. Rowe first began collecting original prints by Alphonse Mucha, Katsushika Hokusai, Honoré Daumier, and Aubrey Beardsley. He then expanded his collection to include Bill Mauldin prints, drawings, and paintings, as well as artifacts, posters, and flags from both World Wars. MoFA was pleased to host two concurrent exhibitions of his collections in 2008: the book illustrations of Hokusai and an exhibition celebrating the two hundredth birthday of Daumier. Patrick Rowe wrote both catalogue texts and his research was the basis for very successful outreach and onsite programs at the Museum of Fine Arts.

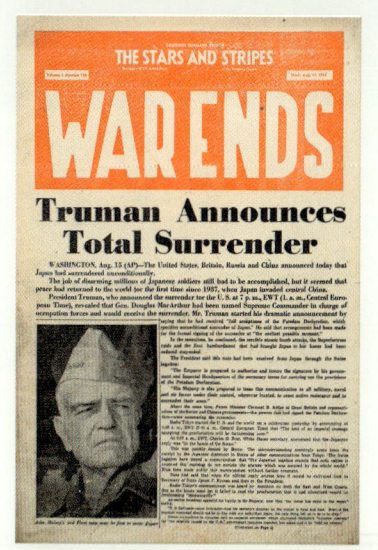

▲ United States Service "Welcome Home" Flag, *c.* 1945. *Inscription*: BULL DOG BUNTING (stamped along the hoist [i.e., the border of the flag nearest to the flagpole]).

◀ Facing page: United States Service and Victory Flag, 1942-1945. *Inscription*: none.

◀ Letter written by Thomas H. Rowe, Staff Sergeant, United States Army Air Force from the Collection of Patrick M. Rowe, Thomas H. Rowe's son.

FLORIDA STATE UNIVERSITY INSTITUTE ON WORLD WAR II

TheRingling
THE JOHN & MABLE RINGLING
MUSEUM OF ART
STATE ART MUSEUM OF FLORIDA | FLORIDA STATE UNIVERSITY

▶ Robert Capa, *Parachute*, March 24, 1945, gelatin silver print, SN11310.18. Gift of Warren J. and Margot Coville. Collection of The John and Mable Ringling Museum of Art, the State Art Museum of Florida, Florida State University, Sarasota, Florida.

WITNESS TO WAR

Selections of Photographic Collections from Florida State University Institute on WWII and The John and Mable Ringling Museum of Art

Christopher A. Jones, Curator

Our understanding of World War II comes from the direct personal accounts of all those who experienced the conflict firsthand. But our collective memory is shaped by the innumerable films and photographs that documented the war. In WWII, the camera became a weapon as instrumental in fighting as any bomb or rifle. The US War Department saw the value of public relations in an American society increasingly dominated by the press.

The US Army, Army Air Forces, and Navy each had their own cadres of photographers that documented the course of the war. Prints were archived, and after review by wartime censors some were selected for release to the press. Images were carefully chosen to have the most impact on morale, both at home and on the front.

The camera was also a tactical instrument. Film and photographs offered strategic reconnaissance, instant tactical maps, a means to calibrate bombs and artillery, and the most efficient way to record and disseminate brute facts. From mundane images cataloguing war *matériel* to heart-wrenching images of battlefield casualties, the camera surveyed all with the same dispassionate gaze.

Yet photography also bears witness to the human presence behind the lens. The pictures displayed here consist of both official military photographs, produced on duty, as well as personal snapshots and candid scenes from the collections of the GIs who took and kept them. Many are creased, dog-eared and discolored, as a result of their history as both military documents and personal mementos. They are not the typical exhibition prints one would expect to find in an art museum, but they are important artifacts that link private memory and our shared history.

The Photojournalists

American photographer William Eugene Smith (1918–1978) and the Hungarian born Robert Capa (1913–1954) both made a name for themselves as war correspondents photographing for *Life* magazine. The two practiced what today is often called "embedded journalism," as they followed units of GIs on the front or even accompanied them behind enemy lines to take riveting photographs for a public eager for images of the war.

Capa's photograph of a wounded paratrooper was taken as part of his photo-essay "The Last Round," an article describing a heroic airborne assault into Germany by the 17th Airborne Division, featured in the April 1945 issue of *Life* magazine. In order to get the story, Capa parachuted in with the 513th Parachute Infantry Regiment on their perilous mission to outflank the enemy from the other side of the Rhine River. His willingness to put himself in harm's way to produce the most dramatic pictures is summed up in his oft-cited personal philosophy, that "If your pictures aren't good enough, you aren't close enough."

▲ *Rear flight deck on carrier*, gelatin silver print. Walter J. and Elaine Duggan Collection of the Institute on WWII, Florida State University.

▲ W. Eugene Smith, *Invasion of Okinawa* (US army tank on battlefield), April 1, 1945, gelatin silver print. SN11310.272. Gift of Warren J. and Margot Coville. Collection of The John and Mable Ringling Museum of Art, the State Art Museum of Florida, Florida State University, Sarasota, Florida.

FLORIDA STATE UNIVERSITY INSTITUTE ON WORLD WAR II

▲ *Asiatic Pacific Campaign ribbon and medal.* Lonnie R. Smith Collection of the Institute on WWII, Florida State University.

▶ W. Eugene Smith, *Okinawa, World War II* (Solider carrying weapon on his shoulder), gelatin silver print, SN11310.273. Gift of Warren J. and Margot Coville. Collection of The John and Mable Ringling Museum of Art, the State Art Museum of Florida, Florida State University, Sarasota, Florida.

Smith got too close to danger while photographing soldiers on the front line in Okinawa in May, 1945, not long after he took these photographs. His goal was to capture what a day in the life of an infantryman was like in the Pacific Theater, but while working, artillery shrapnel struck and seared through his hand and into his face, severely wounding him. It took two years of recovery before he was physically able to use a camera again. These would be his last WWII photos.

Photojournalists working at the front, like Capa and Smith, often sought out the grittier aspects of war, rather than simply parrot the official narratives of the US War Department. However, even though photographers were rarely restricted in what they could photograph, military censors still had final say in what was published. It wasn't until September, 1943, nearly two years into the war that military censors permitted the public to see photographs of US GIs killed in action. Because the armed forces and the press worked so closely together, wartime visual culture was often highly orchestrated.

The Charlotte Dee Mansfield Collection

Charlotte Mansfield (1915–2007) had a passion for photography that resonated throughout her entire life. She was born in Hanford, California, but grew up in Garber, Oklahoma, where her interest in photography was piqued at an early age by watching her father produce tintypes. As a young woman, Mansfield aspired to become a photojournalist. She studied English at the University of Central Oklahoma and regularly submitted news photographs taken with her own Speed Graphic camera to local papers.

Mansfield consistently demonstrated a pioneering spirit. In 1942, she enlisted in the Women's Army Auxiliary Corps (WAAC) just three months after its formation and lent her skills in photography to the war effort. She trained at the Photography School at Lowry Field, Colorado, in 1943 as part of the very first class of women to study aerial photography with the US Army Air Forces. She was deployed to England in 1944 as a sergeant in the restructured Women's Army Corps (WAC), where she served in the Eight Photo Tech Squadron, 325th Photo Wing, Reconnaissance. As an "Air WAC," her duties included developing film and operating photo printers, creating aerial reconnaissance photo mosaics, and photographing operations on base for training pamphlets.

The photographs Mansfield chose to take and collect reflect a unique experience of the war. Images verifying the efficacy of Allied bombing raids are found alongside more intimate and personal snapshots that record the daily lives of fellow WACs as they negotiated the expectations of their new role as women in the military. Evidently, she found military life a suitable fit. After her discharge at the end of WWII, she reenlisted in the WAC, and later the US Air Force, where she served as a photographer until her retirement in 1973. She was an active camera club member and frequent participant in juried photography competitions and completed her Master's degree in journalism in 1983 at age 68.

The James S. Bowns Collection

James Smith Bowns (1918–2001) had a long career in the US Army, serving from his enlistment in 1942 until his retirement in 1967. Bowns was born in Pocatello, Idaho, and lived in the area prior to the war, managing a local movie theater and attending the University of Idaho. This experience qualified him for duty in the Army Signal Corps, where he received training in photography and film production and was assigned to the 167th Signal Photographic Company as a commissioned lieutenant.

The 167th landed in France in September, 1944, and was responsible for documenting, through still photographs and film, the operation to liberate France. They worked as detached units, usually under a lieutenant, and were often granted considerable

▲ *Charlotte Mansfield adjusts a camera at the Lowry Field photography school*, Colorado, 1943, gelatin silver print. Charlotte Mansfield Collection of the Institute on WWII, Florida State University.

▲ *Lt. James S. Bowns*, November 1944, gelatin silver print. James S. Bowns Collection of the Institute on WWII, Florida State University.

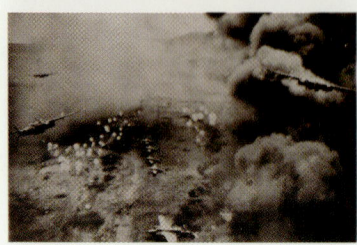

FLORIDA STATE UNIVERSITY INSTITUTE ON WORLD WAR II

▲ *Bombing crew*, 1943 or 1944, gelatin silver print. Gordon McCraw Collection of the Institute on WWII, Florida State University.

▲ *Bombing run* (Pacific), gelatin silver print. Stephen Winters Collection of the Institute on WWII, Florida State University.

▶ 486th Bombardment Group, 3rd Wing, 8th Air Force. *Members of the Photo Tech Unit, 486th Bombardment Group*, 1944-1945, gelatin silver print, SN11332.536. Gift of Warren J. and Margot Coville. Collection of The John and Mable Ringling Museum of Art, the State Art Museum of Florida, Florida State University, Sarasota, Florida.

▶ 486th Bombardment Group, 3rd Wing, 8th Air Force. *Aerial view of the bombing of a Luftwaffe Base in Rechlin, Germany, by the 486th Bombardment Group*, September 25, 1944, gelatin silver print, SN11332.283. Gift of Warren J. and Margot Coville. Collection of The John and Mable Ringling Museum of Art, the State Art Museum of Florida, Florida State University, Sarasota, Florida.

WITNESS TO WAR

autonomy and access in covering events during the war. Bowns led one such unit, and he and his men spent time with the 94th and later the 66th Infantry Division as they worked to contain dangerous pockets of German resistance along the Atlantic coast of France. In towns such as Lorient and Sant-Nazaire, the enemy remained entrenched until the very end of the war in Europe. Although Signal Corps photographers had the luxury of coming and going as they pleased, their constant proximity to the front lines meant that they often came under fire.

Bowns continued in the Signal Corps long after the war, serving in Europe and later Korea. He directed numerous films for the Army and ultimately achieved the rank of lieutenant colonel and was one of the producers for *The Big Picture*, a weekly documentary television series from the Army Signal Corps Pictorial Service that chronicled the US military's achievements in WWII and continued role in global affairs. He eventually retired to Tewksbury, New Jersey, where he spent the remainder of his life active in community affairs.

The Warren J. and Margot Coville Collection

The photographs in the Coville Collection demonstrate some of the different ways of seeing that photography generated during the course of the war. This selection, chosen from nearly 500 images, ranges from personal snapshots to technical aerial photographs that Warren (b. 1925) produced as part the 486th Bombardment Group, Eight Air Force, while stationed in Sudbury, England, in 1944 and 1945.

Warren enlisted in the Army just two months after graduating from high school. Having experience as an assistant to a portrait photographer, he was assigned to the Army Air Forces where he trained to fly as an onboard photographer as part of B-17 and B-24 flight crews. One of only four members of his technical unit to have flight clearance, he was on rotation to fly along on bombing missions to targets behind enemy lines. He photographed using a handheld aerial camera while much larger, electronically-controlled cameras were also mounted in a few of the bombers.

For the crewmembers, the eight to ten hour missions were grueling. The men flew unpressurized planes at high altitudes and under harrowing anti-aircraft fire. Warren himself was grazed by searing flak on one flight, but was protected from serious injury by his heavy, insulated flight suit. Even upon landing, the mission's intensity was still not over for the photo tech unit. "The exposed film was the first thing unloaded from the planes when they landed," Warren recalls. "It came off before anyone else, even the injured." The unit worked quickly to process the long rolls of film, then raced the photographs to headquarters for interpretation, often driving at high speeds along country roads at night under blackout conditions, an experience Warren remembers as being nearly as treacherous as the bombing missions themselves.

Warren returned home in October in 1945 and met his future wife Margot, a young Jewish Holocaust survivor taking refuge in Detroit. Warren put his experiences in photography and film processing to use after the war, co-founding ABC Photography, a successful photo-finishing chain that spanned the country for decades. The Covilles retired to the Sarasota area where they still reside.

The Paul K. Dougherty Collection

When Paul K. Dougherty (1914–2002) enlisted in the Army Air Forces at age 18, he was hoping to become a machine gunner aboard the famous B-17 bombers that dominated the skies over Europe. However, when the military learned that this native of Rochester, New York, had worked the night shift at the Eastman Kodak Company's film emulsion laboratories, it was decided that his knowledge of photography was more

▲ *Planes overhead*, gelatin silver print. Stephen Winters Collection of the Institute on WWII, Florida State University.

▲ *Aerial view of Ulm, Germany, after Allied bombing on December 17, 1944*, gelatin silver print. Charlotte Mansfield Collection of the Institute on WWII, Florida State University.

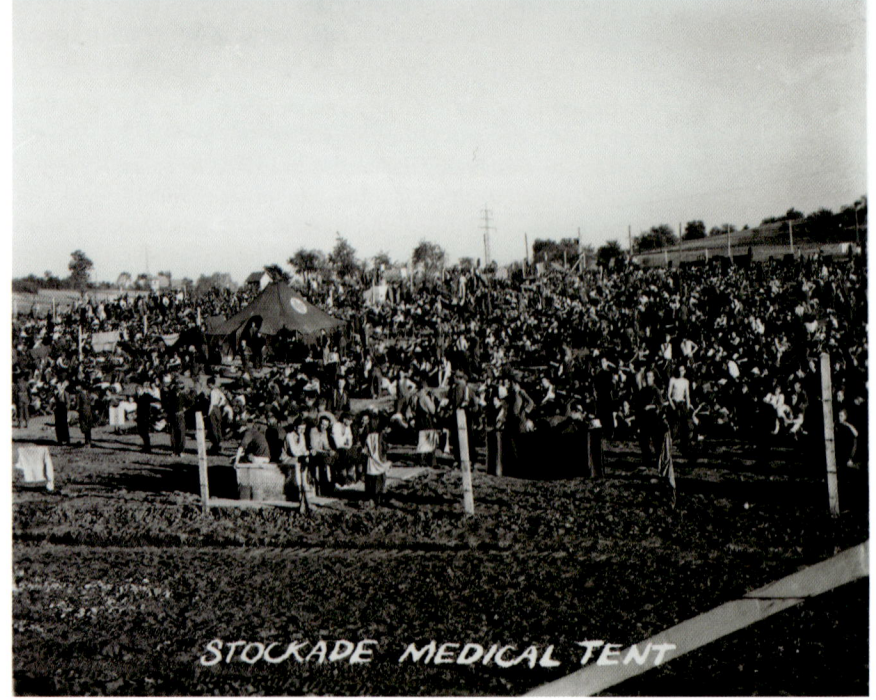

FLORIDA STATE UNIVERSITY INSTITUTE ON WORLD WAR II

▲ *Remnants of the "Volksstrum,"* May 15, 1945, gelatin silver print. Paul K. Dougherty Collection of the Institute on WWII, Florida State University.

▲ *Daily water rations*, May 15, 1945, gelatin silver print. Paul K. Dougherty Collection of the Institute on WWII, Florida State University.

▶ *A prayer is said*, gelatin silver print. Paul K. Dougherty Collection of the Institute on WWII, Florida State University.

▶ *Stockade medical tent*, 1945, gelatin silver print. Paul K. Dougherty Collection of the Institute on WWII, Florida State University.

68

valuable to the war effort than his gunnery skills. As a result, he was diverted to the Army Signal Corps, where he would see much more of the war than he could have imagined.

Dougherty's course of training brought him to Dale Mabry Army Airfield in Tallahassee, where he learned procedures for running battlefield darkrooms that could rapidly develop and print photographs in difficult situations, a skill-set requiring great adaptability and ingenuity that he put into practice. He also studied techniques in aerial photography and flew aboard P-38s on photo-reconnaissance missions as part of the Ninth Air Force's support of Allied ground troops liberating Western Europe.

Dougherty transferred to the Third Army, led by General George S. Patton, on its epic advance across Europe to deliver the final blow to the German army. There he served as a technical sergeant in a pool of photographers whose task was to document actions as they unfolded. His rank and photographer's badge gave him wide access to the theater of operations. From the Battle of the Bulge and into Germany, Austria, and the liberation of Czechoslovakia, he witnessed some of the pivotal moments in modern history through the camera lens.

Dougherty's collection also includes images of some of humanity's most unspeakable atrocities. He was among those to witness the conditions of concentration camps after their liberation and worked to gather photographic evidence used to prosecute Nazi war criminals at the Nuremberg Trials. These images have captured the unbearable cruelty of the Holocaust for posterity and recorded the individuals who beheld its trauma firsthand.

In 1998, Dougherty decided to discard the hundreds of WWII photographs he had held for over fifty years, assuming that no one would be interested in these personal artifacts. He had already begun setting them out for the trash when his son Kevin intervened. The two met with Dr. William Oldson at Florida State University and donated the photos as one of the founding collections of the Institute on World War II and the Human Experience.

The Walter J. and Elaine Duggan Collection

Walter J. (1915–1996) and his wife Elaine Duggan both served in the war, she in the Women's Army Corps and he in the US Navy Reserves as a Photographer's Mate. Walter spent much of his time assigned to the Advance Headquarters of Admiral Chester W. Nimitz, Commander-in-Chief of the Pacific Fleet (CINCPAC). As such, he was stationed in Guam, Saipan, Iwo Jima, and eventually Tokyo. He shot color 16mm film from the *USS Bunker Hill* and the *USS Monitor*. He was also assigned to various CINCPAC Combat Photographic Units tasked with documenting naval combat and operations.

These units, drawn from pools of capable still and motion picture photographers, were directed by Captain Edward Steichen, perhaps the most well-known photographer in the United States at the time. Using skills from his long career as an art and fashion photographer, Steichen coordinated placement of photographic units and personally reviewed and approved material, with the over-arching goal of presenting a heroic, if propagandized, image of the Navy's efforts to the US public. The results included films such as *The Fighting Lady* and the *Power in the Pacific* exhibition at the Museum of Modern Art in New York, both in 1945.

Duggan filmed the epic Battle of Okinawa as part of a seven man Special Photography Unit deployed across the task force group, filming aboard the *USS Astoria* while Steichen directed the photographic operations from the carrier *USS Lexington*. The fleet came under a barrage of *kamikaze* attacks as the Japanese mobilized a last ditch effort to stave off an invasion by US forces. Duggan stayed on deck in difficult and dangerous

▲ *Paul K. Dougherty in front of the Arc de Triomphe*, 1944, gelatin silver print. Paul K. Dougherty Collection of the Institute on WWII, Florida State University.

▲ *Living room window — Hitler's Hideout*, 1945, gelatin silver print. Paul K. Dougherty Collection of the Institute on WWII, Florida State University.

FLORIDA STATE UNIVERSITY INSTITUTE ON WORLD WAR II

▲ *Lab operations in Leyte group photo*, November 1944, gelatin silver print. Stephen Winters Collection of the Institute on WWII, Florida State University.

▲ *Stephen Winters in front of the 8th Photo Tech Unit lab*, 1943-1945. Stephen Winters Collection of the Institute on WWII, Florida State University.

▶ *Drying film the quick way*, c. 1942-1944, gelatin silver print. Gordon McCraw Collection of the Institute on WWII, Florida State University.

▶ *Staff Sergeant McCraw with photo history*, c. 1942-1944, gelatin silver print. Gordon McCraw Collection of the Institute on WWII, Florida State University.

circumstances filming the incoming enemy planes as defending gunners frantically tried to knock them down. For his efforts, Steichen commended him for his "contribution to the visual records of the war" while in the line of fire. The film shot by Duggan and his comrades during that battle was used in the short films *The Fleet that Came to Stay* (1945) and *To the Shores of Iwo Jima* (1945).

The Gordon D. McCraw Collection

The Virginia-born Gordon D. McCraw (1913–2005) joined the Army in 1934, well before the war, in order to supplement his income during the Great Depression. Stationed with the Third Army Air Corps in his hometown of Lynchburg, McCraw trained in operations and intelligence and advanced to the rank of staff sergeant. When the United States entered the war in 1941, he was transferred to the photography technical unit of the newly activated 405th Bomb Squadron of the 38th Bomb Group, comprised of B-25 "Mitchells." By August 1942, he was deployed to Australia, where the Fifth Air Force took its part in the arduous reclamation of the southwest Pacific from the Japanese.

The snapshots and photographs from McCraw's collection offer an insight into the daily life of the 38th Bomb Group. As pilots flew daringly low bombing and strafing runs on enemy positions, photographers on board captured the action, thereby providing invaluable tactical information on the accuracy of the attacks and the layout of the terrain below. Back on base, snapshots and portraits recorded the particularities of remote and often rugged conditions as the men moved from Australia to Papua New Guinea, the Philippines and onward. Often the photographic technical unit had to improvise in running a photo lab in less than hospitable environs, as in the case of expediting the drying of processed film by rolling it out under the sun.

In an interview from 1998, McCraw recalled that life at war was always shadowed by danger, both real and expected. He mentioned that, on more than one occasion, he was under machinegun fire from incoming Japanese fighter planes. However, he went on to stress how remarkable his experiences were, and how much he enjoyed meeting and trading with the people of Papua New Guinea. Many of the photos of this collection mark these improbable cross-cultural encounters.

The Stephen Winters Collection

New Yorker Stephen S. Winters (1920–2003) had completed four years of college when he enlisted in the Army Air Forces in 1942. He served as a photographer with the Eight Photo Tech Lab Section Advanced Detachment, and the 91st Photo Wing, Reconnaissance, of the Fifth Air Force. Winters traveled with this advanced echelon as they were stationed first in New Guinea, then the Netherlands East Indies, the Philippines, Okinawa, and finally Japan, as the Allied forces under the command of General Douglas MacArthur fought their way to the Japanese home islands.

The 91st Photo Wing was responsible for supplying the Fifth Air Force with aerial reconnaissance photographs of the innumerable islands and shorelines in the region, thereby providing more up-to-date strategic maps and supply targets for tactical operations. The pilots flew risky missions over enemy targets in planes that were unarmed in order to accommodate photographic equipment and maximize their range. These reconnaissance flights also sought out downed pilots, wounded personnel, and POWs to facilitate rescue operations.

Winter's collection of photographs is noteworthy because it creates a personal, visual record of the historic advance of the Fifth Air Force. His scenic landscapes, candid shots of rest and creative entertainment offer an image of the unique culture of life at war.

▲*Sergeant Rhode with local New Guinea children*, 1944, silver gelatin print. Stephen Winters Collection of the Institute on WWII, Florida State University.

▲*Japanese officer*, gelatin silver print. Stephen Winters Collection of the Institute on WWII, Florida State University.

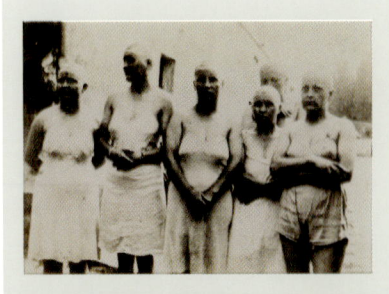

FLORIDA STATE UNIVERSITY INSTITUTE ON WORLD WAR II

▲ *Shorn female collaborators*, 1944-1945, gelatin silver print. Paul K. Dougherty Collection of the Institute on WWII, Florida State University.

▲ *Don't fraternize sign*, gelatin silver print. William Auld Collection of the Institute on WWII, Florida State University.

▶ Robert Capa, *Shorn Collaborator*, August 18, 1944, gelatin silver print, SN11310.17. Gift of Warren J. and Margot Coville. Collection of The John and Mable Ringling Museum of Art, the State Art Museum of Florida, Florida State University, Sarasota, Florida.

▶ *Hitler youth*, May 15, 1945, gelatin silver print. Paul K. Dougherty Collection of the Institute on WWII, Florida State University.

72

The collection is also intriguing for its representations of Japanese people, from dejected soldiers taken prisoners of war, to more idyllic scenes of women in traditional kimonos. This surprising clutch of photographs perhaps hints at a nuanced meditation on the nature of "the enemy."

After the war, Winters pursued advanced study and eventually taught Geology at Florida State University for many years.

Witness to War at the Ringling

The photography exhibition was realized in collaboration with the Institute on World War II and the Human Experience, Florida State University. The Institute is one of the largest repositories of material from WWII veterans. Its archive of over six thousand collections includes many of the objects here on display. The research, resources and logistical assistance provided by the Institute were invaluable in the exhibition's success at the Ringling.

Witness to War at the Ringling was part of Legacy of Valor, a campaign that rallies our community to honor veterans, inspire patriotism and embrace freedom. A mosaic of community-driven partnerships are created to educate, build enthusiasm and focus the community to use time, talent and treasure to recognize the service and sacrifice of all veterans throughout the campaign and beyond.

Christopher A. Jones is the Assistant Curator of Exhibitions at the John and Mable Ringling Museum of Art. He holds a Master of Arts in Art History from the University of New Mexico and is a PhD candidate in Art History at the University of Florida.

Suggestions for Further Reading

Maslowski, Peter. *Armed with Cameras: the American Military Photographers of World War II*. New York: Free Press, 1993.

Soule, Thayer. *Shooting the Pacific War: Marine Corps Combat Photography in WWII*. Lexington: University of Kentucky Press, 2000.

Sumners, Charles Eugene, and Ann Sumners. *Darkness Visible: Memoir of a World War II Combat Photographer*. Jefferson, N.C.: McFarland, 2002.

Thompson, George Raynor. *The Signal Corps: The Test (December 1941 to July 1943)*. Washington: Office of the Chief of Military History, Dept. of the Army, 1957.

▲ *Japanese women*, 1945, gelatin silver print. Stephen Winters Collection of the Institute on WWII, Florida State University.

▲ *Japanese Red Cross nurses*, 1945, gelatin silver print. Stephen Winters Collection of the Institute on WWII, Florida State University.

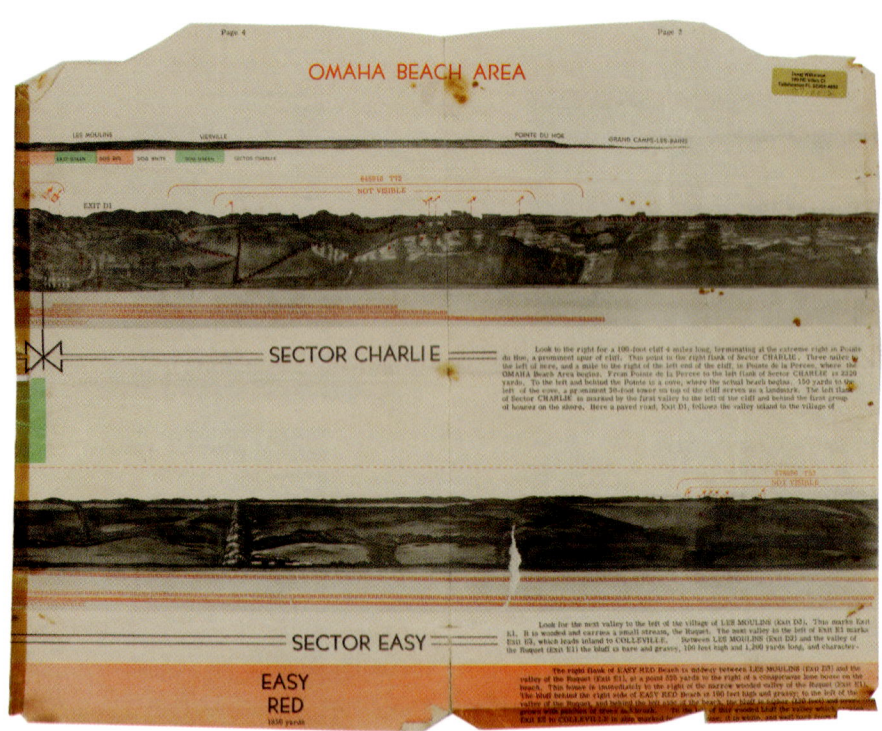

▲ *79th Infantry Division Cross of the Lorraine Division shoulder patch.* Charles Stripling Collection of the Institute on WWII, Florida State University.

▶ *Chart of advance preparations for landing at Omaha Beach.* The preparations for D-Day can be seen here on a chart extracted from a larger booklet that was given to troops who were to be part of the invading forces at Normandy. The booklet was entitled "Defenses as of May 14, 1944." The pages include various charts and indicate the topographical features of the beach sectors (Easy, Fox and Charlie) at Omaha Beach. The descriptions include the location of high and low tide, vegetation, gradients, structures, cliffs, the distance to nearby towns and access to high ground. There are sections on airplane recognition, the order of assault, naval gunfire support and aerial bombardment. Douglas Wilkinson Collection of the Institute on WWII, Florida State University.

Doug Wilkinson enlisted in the United States Naval Reserve in 1943, serving in the European Theater. His unit helped supply Omaha Beach during D-Day landings. Wilkinson was honorably discharged on January 26, 1946.

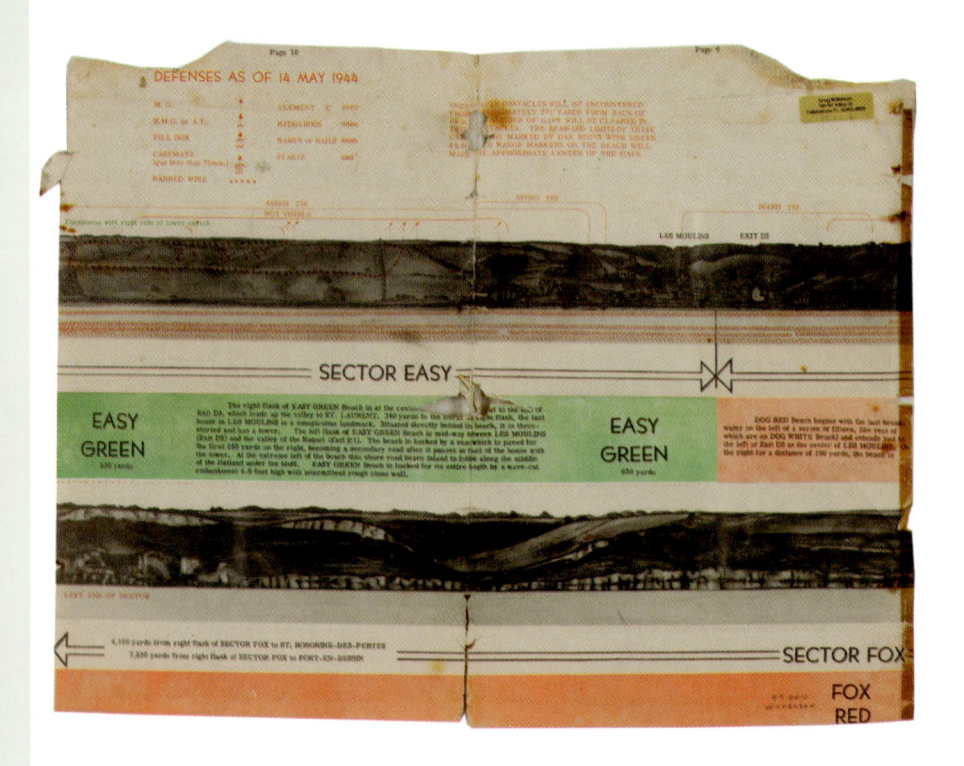

THE HUMAN EXPERIENCE

A GLIMPSE OF THE COLLECTIONS OF THE INSTITUTE ON WORLD WAR II

The focus of the Institute on World War II and the Human Experience is collecting and preserving the memories of the men and women who participated in all the military branches, service with the Merchant Marine, Red Cross, USO, workers and volunteers on the Home Front during the WWII era and the immediate postwar period (i.e., 1939 - 1949). With over 6,000 collections and growing, the Institute on WWII has items from individuals and units presenting all states and a few from other nations. The Institute's collections are used in exhibits, papers and dissertations from college students from Florida and other states, documentaries, news articles, books, genealogy research, public school classrooms and projects.

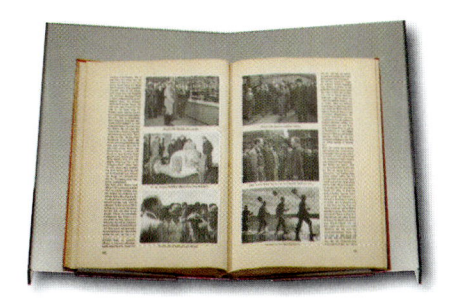

Among the items collected from the European Theater are these "cigarette books." "Cigarette books" are examples of German propaganda. The books were sold to the public with text but no photographs or images. Cigarette and tobacco companies would sell numbered photographic prints in cigarette packs that corresponded with blank numbered spaces in the books. It was up to the consumer of the cigarettes to coordinate the numbers and glue the photographs into the books. There were a variety of such cigarette books published in Germany during the war.

The book on the left was used to celebrate the charisma and grand leadership of the Führer, Adolf Hitler. The photographs show Hitler in the most positive light as he is seen interacting as the supreme leader with dignitaries, citizens, the military and Hitler Youth.

The book on the right was dedicated to the Wehrmacht, the unified armed forces of Germany from 1935 to 1946. It consisted of the Heer (the Army), the Kriegsmarine (the Navy) and the Luftwaffe or Air Force. The Nazis eventually dominated over three million square kilometers of territory, an accomplishment made possible by the combined military forces of Germany, with the Wehrmacht bearing the brunt of the efforts to secure conquered territory. The focus of this cigarette book is on the military might and successes of the German Third Reich. The sketches that have been attached to the pages are colorful and consistent throughout. They illustrate propaganda efforts used by the Nazi regime to convince the German people of their superiority and their military might.

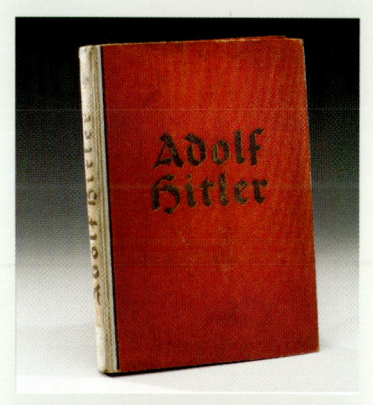

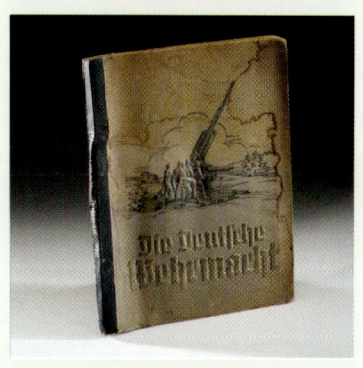

▲ *Cigarette books* from the Collections of Gilbert W. Johnson and Paul K. Dougherty at the Institute on WWII, Florida State University.

Gilbert Johnson was in the US Navy and was stationed in the Caribbean, China, Europe and the Pacific. Paul K. Dougherty served as a photographer (see page 14 sidebar).

75

FLORIDA STATE UNIVERSITY INSTITUTE ON WORLD WAR II

▲ *42nd Infantry Division patch.* Lonnie Lonzalo Cannon Collection of the Institute on WWII, Florida State University.

▶ *Advance of the 7th Division maps.* The commemorative maps here illustrate the movement of the 71st Division from Le Havre, France, through Germany and into Austria. Note that the division's most significant engagements are prominently marked on the maps. Giles Jared Patterson Collection of the Institute on WWII, Florida State University.

Giles Patterson was from Jacksonville, Florida, and attended Officer's Candidate School at Fort Sill, Oklahoma. He later served as a supply officer with the 608th Battalion, 71st Division, in Europe.

▶ *Flight Log Book.* Carl O. Dunbar Collection of the Institute on WWII, Florida State University.

▶ Facing page: *Jewish Prayer Book of Leon Lindauer.* The Siddur, Hebrew for prayer book, was distributed to service members of the Jewish faith. Leon Lindauer, from Savannah, Georgia, served in the US Army's Company F, 351st Infantry, 88th Infantry Division. He was killed in action in Italy on September 28, 1944. Leon Lindauer Collection of the Institute on WWII, Florida State University

▶ Facing page: *Bible.* This copy of the New Testament was given to Charles Stripling during basic training at Camp Crowder, Missouri in 1942. These were distributed by the camp chaplain and contained a message to the troops from President Franklin D. Roosevelt on the first page. The President not only wrote introductions to the Protestant testament, but also to those issued to Roman Catholics and Jews. Charles Stripling Collection of the Institute on WWII, Florida State University.

Charles Stripling joined the 327th Engineer Combat Battalion in March 1943, and later served in the European Theater. He was discharged at Camp Gordon, Georgia in 1945.

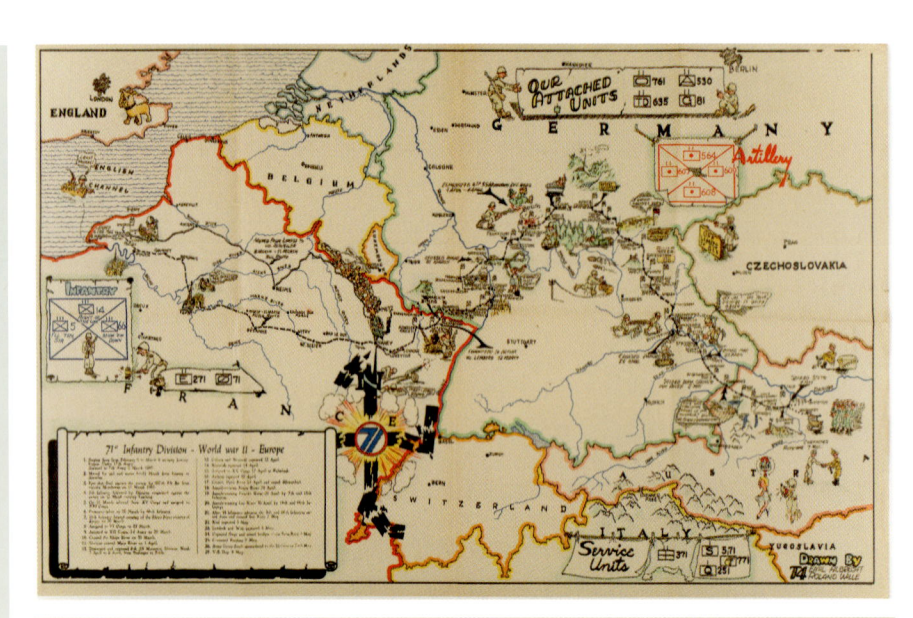

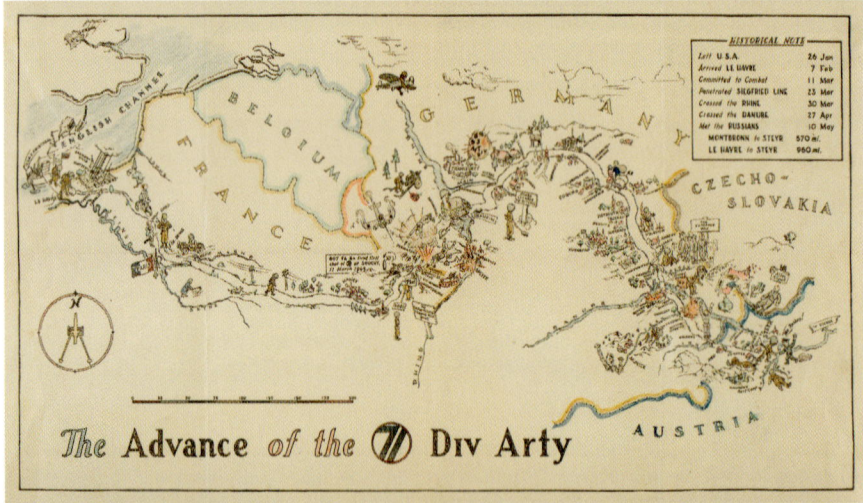

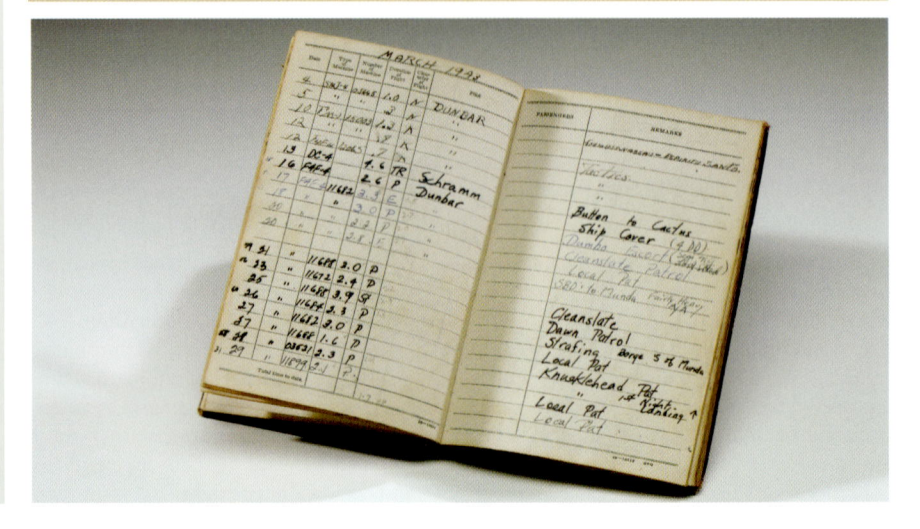

THE HUMAN EXPERIENCE

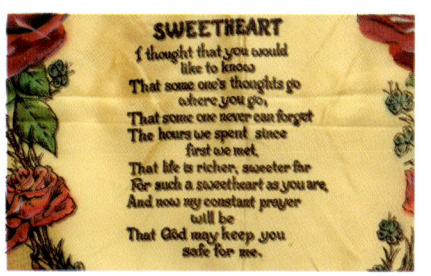

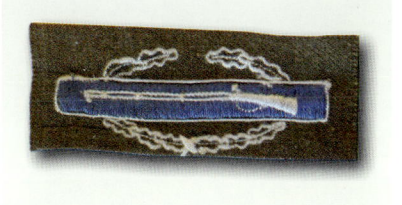

◂ *Rifle and Combat Infantry patch.* Lonnie Lonzalo Cannon Collection of the Institute on WWII, Florida State University.

◂ *Group photo including Robert Watson* who was inducted into the US Army at Pittsburgh, Pennsylvania, in July 1943. He was assigned to the 316th Port Company of the 511th Port Battalion where he was a hatch foreman and squad leader loading and unloading cargo ships and landing craft, and he served in the South Pacific from 1943 to 1946. Robert Watson Collection of the Institute on WWII, Florida State University.

◂ *Items used by Loren Fink during his time as a POW in Germany.* Loren Fink Collection of the Institute on WWII, Florida State University.

Loren Fink served in the 366th Bomb Squadron, 8th Air Force, and participated in several bombing campaigns over Normandy, Northern France, and Central Europe. On October 14, 1943, during a campaign over the German city of Schweinfurt, Fink was shot down and taken as a Prisoner of War. Fink would remain a POW for nineteen months and nine days until being turned over to the American Army in Halle, Germany nine days before the end of the war. Fink would later be discharged on November 15, 1945.

◂ *Pillow cover.* This pillow cover, a souvenir from Bainbridge Air Field, Georgia, was one of six such covers Senter sent to his fiancée back home. She kept them in a trunk with mementos until her death, after which they were returned to the Senter family who donated some of the items to the Institute on World War II. Pillow covers like this one were very popular souvenirs with service men. They did not break, and were easy to tuck into a duffle bag or mailing envelope. Ernest Senter Collection of the Institute on WWII, Florida State University.

Ernest Senter was a B-17 pilot in the 388th Bomb Group, 8th Air Force, stationed in Leicester, England. His plane was shot down over Beckdorf, Germany, in December of 1944, killing five crew members including himself.

FLORIDA STATE UNIVERSITY INSTITUTE ON WORLD WAR II

▲ *Prisoner of war artworks.* Fred H. Taeger Collection of the Institute on WWII, Florida State University.

Fred H. Taeger served in the US Army from 1943 to 1946, during which time he worked as a German interpreter at Camp Forrest, Tennessee. He was assigned to the intelligence section of the POW area and directed the interrogation of German POWs. Taeger acted as interpreter and assembled records detailing their backgrounds. While serving at Camp Forrest, Taeger received and collected art work created by German POWs.

▶ *Russian band drafted by German Army*, 1945, gelatin silver print. Paul K. Dougherty Collection of the Institute on WWII, Florida State University.

▶ *Christmas*, gelatin silver print. Charlotte Mansfield Collection of the Institute on WWII, Florida State University.

▶ *V-E Day celebration*, Nuremberg, 1945, gelatin silver print. Paul K. Dougherty Collection of the Institute on WWII, Florida State University.

▶ *First decent meal in eleven months*, 1943 or 1944, gelatin silver print. Gordon McCraw Collection of the Institute on WWII, Florida State University.

78

THE HUMAN EXPERIENCE

▲ *Australian soldier crouches behind an armored vehicle*, c. 1942-1944, gelatin silver print. Gordon McCraw Collection of the Institute on WWII, Florida State University.

▲ *Soldiers carry a litter*, c. 1942-1944, gelatin silver print. Gordon McCraw Collection of the Institute on WWII, Florida State University.

▲ *Destroyed boat hulls on the coast of Ceram Island, Indonesia*, c. 1944, gelatin silver print. Gordon McCraw Collection of the Institute on WWII, Florida State University.

◄ *Attacking enemy shipping*, c. 1944, gelatin silver print. Gordon McCraw Collection of the Institute on WWII, Florida State University.

◄ *16-inch guns firing from an Iowa class battleship*, 1944 or 1945, gelatin silver print. Walter J. and Elaine Duggan Collection of the Institute on WWII, Florida State University.

FLORIDA STATE UNIVERSITY INSTITUTE ON WORLD WAR II

▲ *Pacific surrender*, gelatin silver print. Walter J. and Elaine Dugan Collection of the Institute on WWII, Florida State University.

▲ *Japanese delegation arriving aboard the* USS Missouri, *September 2, 1945,* gelatin silver print. Walter J. and Elaine Duggan Collection of the Institute on WWII, Florida State University.

▶ *Going in,* Angaur, 1944, gelatin silver print. Walter J. and Elaine Duggan Collection of the Institute on WWII, Florida State University.

▶ *Men on landing craft*, Southwest Pacific Theater, 1944-1945, gelatin silver print. Stephen Winters Collection of the Institute on WWII, Florida State University.

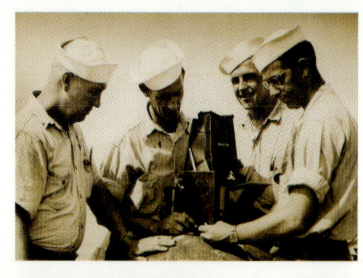

THE HUMAN EXPERIENCE

▲ *Four sailors with a Graflex camera*, 1944-1945, gelatin silver print. Walter J. and Elaine Duggan Collection of the Institute on WWII, Florida State University.

▲ *Soldier using a multiprinter*, 1944 or 1945, gelatin silver print. Charlotte Mansfield Collection of the Institute on WWII, Florida State University.

◀ *"We trade salt, razor blades, old shirts, pants, etc."* 1943-1944, gelatin silver print. Gordon McCraw Collection of the Institute on WWII, Florida State University.

◀ *GIs filming a performer in New Guinea*, c. 1944, gelatin silver print. Stephen Winters Collection of the Institute on WWII, Florida State University.

◀ *Rita McDonald — Film Library*, 1944 or 1945, gelatin silver print. Charlotte Mansfield Collection of the Institute on WWII, Florida State University.

◀ *Japanese soldiers with camouflage*, gelatin silver print. Stephen Winters Collection of the Institute on WWII, Florida State University.

81

FLORIDA STATE UNIVERSITY INSTITUTE ON WORLD WAR II

▲ *Marine Fighting Squadron 231 patch.* Helen Losik and Frank Brickley Collection of the Institute on WWII, Florida State University.

▶ *Returning flight.* Charlotte Mansfield Collection of the Institute on WWII, Florida State University.

▶ *Miss Liberty*, a B-24 bomber, 1943-1945, gelatin silver print. Stephen Winters Collection of the Institute on WWII, Florida State University.

▶ *Nazi helmet and belt buckle.* Dr. Louis S. Moore Collection of the Institute on WWII, Florida State University.

The German Nazi belt buckle is of steel construction and has a pebbled surface. It includes two ropes forming the central design filled in with an eagle clutching the emblematic swastika. The words "GOTT MIT UNS" between the circular ropes translates to "God With Us." The Nazi helmet has a bullet hole at the front and an exit opening at the back that would indicate that the soldier wearing it suffered a deadly head wound. A small stain on the helmet liner appears to be blood. The lack of a unit decal on the helmet indicates that it is probably an M1942 German helmet that never received a factory branch insignia. Such helmets are typically found with a 1943 or 1944 date on the helmet liner band. This one has only the number 58 on the liner band that may be the lot number of its production group.

Little is known of Dr. Louis Moore's experiences during World War II as his collection was delivered to the Institute on World War II by a third party. From the artifacts in his collection, it is apparent that he served in the European Theater.

▶ *Shrapnel.* These examples of shrapnel were donated by Vahnan Ouzoovian, who served in the European Theater of Operations. They include anti-aircraft shells of British manufacture, a rib from a V-1 "buzz bomb," parts from a German V-2 rocket and flak, all found in London. Vahnan Ouzoovian Collection of the Institute on WWII, Florida State University.

THE HUMAN EXPERIENCE

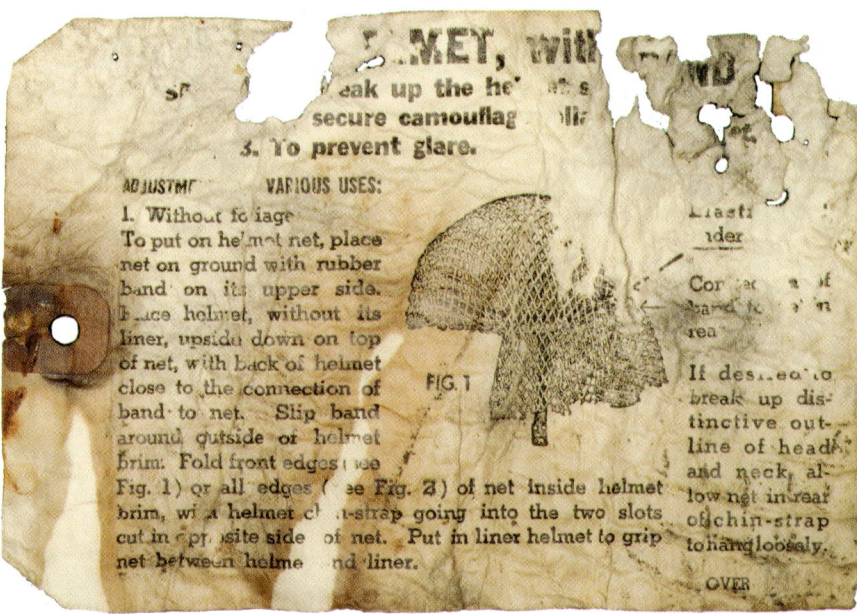

◄ *Cigarette lighter.* John F. Serio Collection of the Institute on WWII, Florida State University. John F. Serio was inducted into the Army Air Forces on October 6, 1942 and served in New Guinea and Southern Philippines as a cryptographic technician. The cigarette case was made from the metal of a downed Japanese plane by an Australian soldier, who gave it to Serio in New Guinea in 1942. Serio was honorably discharged on December 5, 1945.

◄ *Gas can*: this type of gas can was sometimes called a "jerry" can or "jeep" can. The markings on the can indicate that it was made in 1943. William Taylor found this military-issue gas can in his grandfather's garage. The extent of his grandfather's service in World War II is unknown. William H. Taylor Collection of the Institute on WWII, Florida State University.

◄ *GI helmet with green netting and information tag*. Randall Watson Collection of the Institute on WWII, Florida State University. Netting or mesh was used on the helmets for various reasons. It was attached to the helmet by a rubber band with the edges either tucked into the helmet or hanging loosely. The netting helped reduce the glare reflecting off the surface of the helmet. With the netting loosely draped below the rubber band, the shape of the head, face and neck were less obvious to the enemy. The netting was also used to attach foliage to the helmet for camouflage. The instructions that came with the helmet netting warned the soldiers "to avoid wearing too much camouflage foliage at a time on helmet." Randall Watson, whose father was a ball turret gunner during World War II, grew up listening to his father's stories about the war. As an adult, he became a collector of World War II memorabilia some of which he has donated to the Institute on World War II. His collection, including this camouflage M-1940 steel helmet with mesh covering, contains items from various military services.

◄ *GI helmet liner and helmet (liner on left)*. William K. Dyer Collection of the Institute on WWII, Florida State University.

83

FLORIDA STATE UNIVERSITY INSTITUTE ON WORLD WAR II

▶ *Ration books and stamps.* LuVenna Wall Collection of the Institute on WWII, Florida State University.

The extensive commitments of the United States to her military and her Allies across the globe resulted in many shortages of everyday items such as rubber, metal, clothing, and a number of foods The most problematic was food, and it was in short supply for a variety of reasons: much of the processed and canned foods was reserved for shipping overseas to the military and our Allies; transportation of fresh foods was limited due to gasoline and tire rationing, and the priority was the transporting of soldiers and war supplies; foreign foods, such as sugar and coffee, were limited due to restrictions on importing.

Because of these shortages, the US government's Office of Price Administration established a system of rationing that would more fairly distribute foods that were in short supply.

More than 8,000 ration boards across the country administered the program, and every American on the home front was issued a series of ration books during the war. The ration books contained removable stamps redeemable for certain items, like sugar, meat, cooking oil, and canned goods.

▶ *China-India-Burma Theater patch.* Hazel L. Bowman Collection of the Institute on WWII, Florida State University.

▶ *US Marine Pacific Air Wing Headquarters patch.* Helen Losik and Frank Brickley Collection of the Institute on WWII, Florida State University.

▶ *China-India-Burma Red Cross patch.* Hazel L. Bowman Collection of the Institute on WWII, Florida State University.

▶ *Letter home.* Anne and Wayne Coloney Collection of the Institute on WWII, Florida State University.

Wayne H. Coloney joined the US Army in 1943, continuing his family's tradition of military service that dates back to the Revolutionary War. He served with the Hell Cat tank division on the European front, fighting the German army in France and Germany. Coloney was honorably discharged in 1946.

The letter shown here was from Coloney's father, "Pop," who was serving in the Pacific. The letter includes family and weather news as well as comments on the Battle of Iwo Jima. He closes the letter by expressing the love and pride he has for his son Wayne.

84

THE HUMAN EXPERIENCE

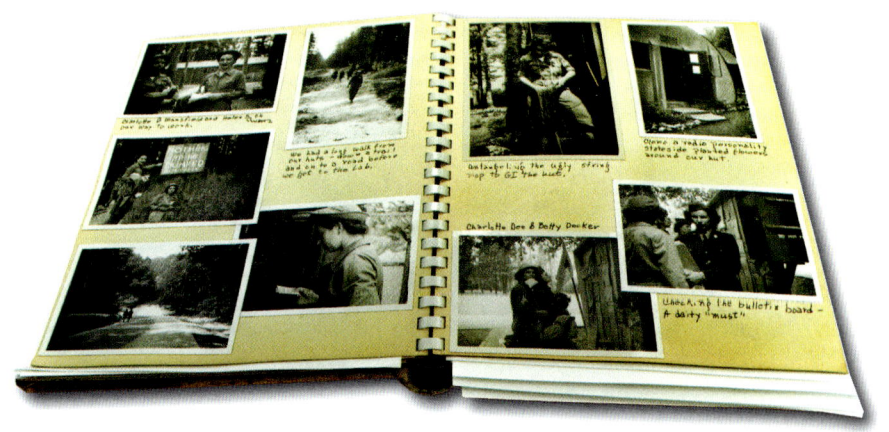

◄ *Ruptured Duck patch*. William Newman Collection of the Institute on WWII, Florida State University.

◄ *Frank Sinatra poster*. This Frank Sinatra poster is from the collection of Brigadier General Walter B. Larew of the United States Army Signal Corps. Larew was the signal officer of a Fighter Command in the Panama Canal Zone. The poster instructed Allied airmen not to sing or count numbers when in contact with the Homing Station: just one steady hum would allow the Homing Station crew to "bring them in." Brigadier General Walter B. Larew Collection of the Institute on WWII, Florida State University.

◄ *Lt. Taffy Logan*, color pencil drawing. Mildred Shearer Collection of the Institute on WWII, Florida State University.

Mildred Shearer was under contract with the USO to travel to military hospitals and create portraits of service personnel recovering from illness or war related injuries. Originally from California, Shearer served in the USO for three years. The portraits were photographed and then the negative, one print and the original drawings were all sent to the subject. They were intended to increase the morale of the troops. The Institute's collection holds 400 portraits created by Shearer.

◄ *Photo album*, c. 1943-1944. Charlotte Mansfield Collection of the Institute on WWII, Florida State University.

◄ Pol Van Geel, *Caricatures of serviceman and woman*. Pol Van Geel Collection of the Institute on WWII, Florida State University.

Pol "Bob" Van Geel was a Dutch caricaturist who immigrated to the United States in 1938. He quickly found work drawing caricatures at college sororities and fraternities. When the United States entered the war in 1941, Van Geel attempted to volunteer but was turned down due to his age, marital status, and the fact that he had a child. Because of the war, finding work as an artist in his home state of New York became difficult as most of his clients had either been drafted or volunteered. Van Geel eventually made his way to Florida, where he drew caricatures of the servicemen and women stationed at military bases in the state.

85

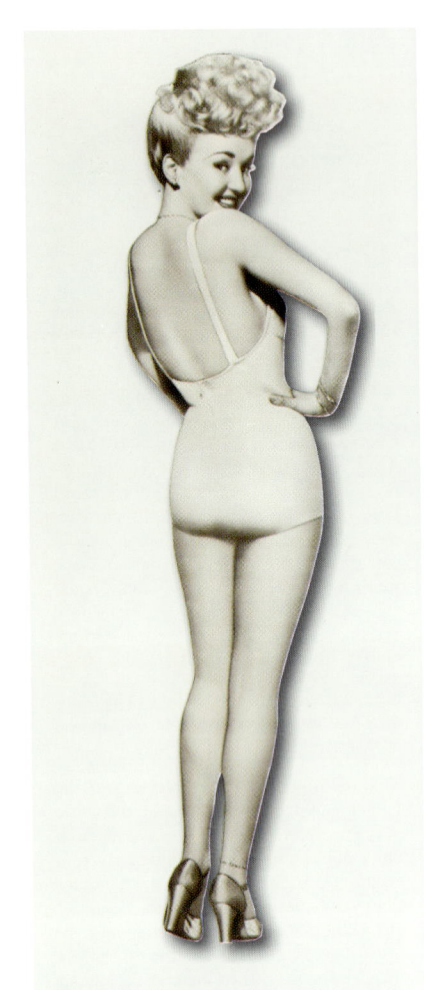

▲ *Betty Grable cutout.* Margaret Salm Collection of the Institute on WWII, Florida State University.

▶ *They all laughed…*, c. 1942-1944, gelatin silver print. Gordon McCraw Collection of the Institute on WWII, Florida State University.

▶ *Entertainers getting ready and the performance of the Five Star Theater*, 1944-1945, gelatin silver print. Stephen Winters Collection of the Institute on WWII, Florida State University.

▶ Facing page: *To a Swell Fellow in the Air Corps! Bet this is the Longest Letter you ever got!* This "Long Letter," sent to Loren Fink in November 1942, is an example of a commercially made, pre-printed letter made to look handwritten. It is a little over five feet in length. Its humorous content was intended to raise the morale of the soldier who received it. Loren Fink Collection of the Institute on WWII, Florida State University.

THE HUMAN EXPERIENCE

▲ *Piano duet*, 38th Bomb Group, c. 1942-1944, gelatin silver print. Gordon McCraw Collection of the Institute on WWII, Florida State University.

◂ *Soldiers Dancing*. Robert Burns Collection of the Institute on WWII, Florida State University.

Robert Burns served on a Naval Radio Station in San Cristobal, Puerto Rico from 1943 until 1946. During that time, Burns documented much of the quotidian experiences of soldiers on the base, as seen in *Soldiers Shaving / Brushing Their Teeth* (see page 89). His photographs capture the lightheartedness and camaraderie common among soldiers in the mundanity of camp life. Burns also photographed life around local towns as the soldiers intermingled with the natives, as seen in *Soldiers Dancing*.

◂ *Injured Soldiers Playing Cards*. Walter J. and Elaine Duggan Collection of the Institute on WWII, Florida State University.

◂ *Scavera DaHalo Desmond with guitar*, 1943-1944, gelatin silver print. Stephen Winters Collection of the Institute on WWII, Florida State University.

87

▶ *Betty Lombardo*, 1944 or 1945, gelatin silver print. Charlotte Mansfield Collection of the Institute on WWII, Florida State University.

▶ *Quonset huts*, 1944-1945, gelatin silver print. Stephen Winters Collection of the Institute on WWII, Florida State University.

▶ *V-Mail letter home.* George Langford Collection of the Institute on WWII, Florida State University.

The use of V-mail, also known as Victory mail, originated in England with the purpose of miniaturizing specifically designed stationery for military families. Reducing the amount of non-essential goods on transport ships was vitally important to the war effort as valuable cargo space could then be used to move war *matériel*. A single V-mail bag could replace 37 postal mailbags needed to send 150,000 one-page letters. The V-mail stationery, as seen here, when microfilmed, was reduced to a thumbnail size; that film was later sent for processing to a specified receiving station. The final print of the letter was about one-quarter its original size. Each letter was inserted into an appropriately sized envelope and delivered to the addressee.

George Langford was drafted into the US Army in March 1943, where he trained with the 220th Engineer Battalion, 20th Armored Division. Langford was shipped to the European front in October 1944, and later landed at Omaha Beach where he was assigned to the First French Army on the southern front. After the German surrender, Langford was on a ship headed for Japan. When the ship was in the Pacific, Japan surrendered. Langford was honorably discharged in September 1945, just ten days after arriving back in the United States. Langford's letter home is a prime example of the types of letters that many soldiers sent during the war.

▶ *Caveman Warfare*, drawing. One of the most notable pieces of the Duggan collection is a large sketch of a bombing raid transposed as a metaphor of prehistoric caveman activities. Though it is unknown who the artist is (whether it is Elaine Duggan's first or second husband), the drawing puts an ingenious twist on a familiar wartime experience. It is a unique, but powerful example of how soldiers coped with the weight of war, creating an unusual and entertaining perspective on their experiences in combat. Walter J. and Elaine Duggan Collection of the Institute on WWII, Florida State University.

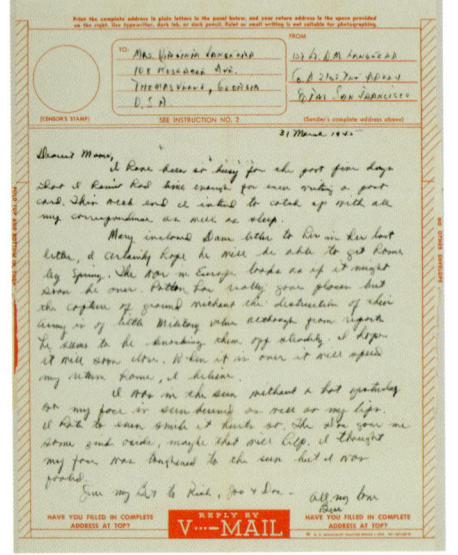

THE HUMAN EXPERIENCE

◀ *No More Tattle Tale Greys*, c. 1942-1944, gelatin silver print. Gordon McCraw Collection of the Institute on WWII, Florida State University.

◀ *GI Toilets*. William Auld Collection of the Institute on WWII, Florida State University.

William R. Auld served as a Captain in the United States 31st Photo Reconnaissance Squadron from 1940 to 1946. His task was to reconnoiter the planned route of General Patton force's and provide him with aerial photos of the terrain and enemy positions. In addition, Auld also spent time detailing the life of soldiers on the march. He recorded daily camp experiences in images such as *GI Toilets*, depicting the soldiers' living facilities and conditions, while simultaneously noting how soldiers spent their free time. Auld photographed the moments leading up to the final days of the war — such as the "Don't Fraternize" sign (on page 72) that warned Americans not to interact with German citizens.

◀ *Soldiers Shaving / Brushing Their Teeth*. Robert Burns Collection of the Institute on WWII, Florida State University.

◀ *Mess kit laundry*, 38th Bomb Group, c. 1942-1943, gelatin silver print. Gordon McCraw Collection of the Institute on WWII, Florida State University.

◀ *Tents on the coast*, 1943-1945, gelatin silver print. Stephen Winters Collection of the Institute on WWII, Florida State University.

◀ *Big Blow*, November 1944, gelatin silver print. Stephen Winters Collection of the Institute on WWII, Florida State University.

◀ *March Field*. Margaret Brocket Collection of the Institute on WWII, Florida State University.

◀ *USO recording*. Phillip Berman Collection of the Institute on WWII, Florida State University.

89

MAJOR BENEFACTORS TO THE INSTITUTE ON WORLD WAR II AND THE HUMAN EXPERIENCE

Department of History, College of Arts and Science, Florida State University

The Institute receives significant budgetary support from Florida State University, including the salaries of the director and staff. Funds from the University also provide the basic office expenses of the Institute, including telephones, postage, and supplies. Private contributions and endowments play a crucial role in allowing the Institute to organize public lectures and conferences, host visiting scholars, fund graduate students and undertake new initiatives to encourage the study and preservation of the history of World War II. We regret in advance any omission: please bring it to the attention of the Institute Director, G. Kurt Piehler at kpiehler@fsu.edu. This list of benefactors is current as of our publication press date of October 1, 2014.

The Doak Campbell Society donors within the President's Club of Florida State University who have made philanthropic contributions of over $100,000:

Anne and John Daves • George and Marian* Langford Endowment in History • Pearl Tyner* • Tom and Meredith Brokaw, Harold Baumgarten and Samuel M. Gibbons Endowed Fund for WWII • Harold Ronson, Harold and Kay Ronson Endowment • Dorothy and Jonathan Rintels, Rintels Professorship of Humanity at the Institute for World War II and the Human Experience

Members of the Robert Strozier Society within the President's Club who have made gifts of greater than $10,000 to the Institute:

TBUF (Tallahassee Branch of the University of Florida) Memorial Endowment Graduate Fellowship • TBUF Memorial Endowed Acquisitions Fund • Ronald Pepper • Ruth K. Shugart • Wilson-Wood Foundation, Inc. • Ben H. Willingham, Jr. • Duane and Betty Bohnstedt 460th Bomb Group (H) Collection

*Members of The James D. Westcott Legacy Society** who have designated the Institute on World War II and the Human Experience in their estate plans to secure the long-term future of the Institute:*

William L. Bailey* • Wayne and Anne* Coloney • Mary Lou G. Madigan* • Ronald Pepper • Sidney L. Monroe, Jr.

*Deceased. **The James D. Westcott Society recognizes individuals who have designated Florida State University as a beneficiary through their estate plans.

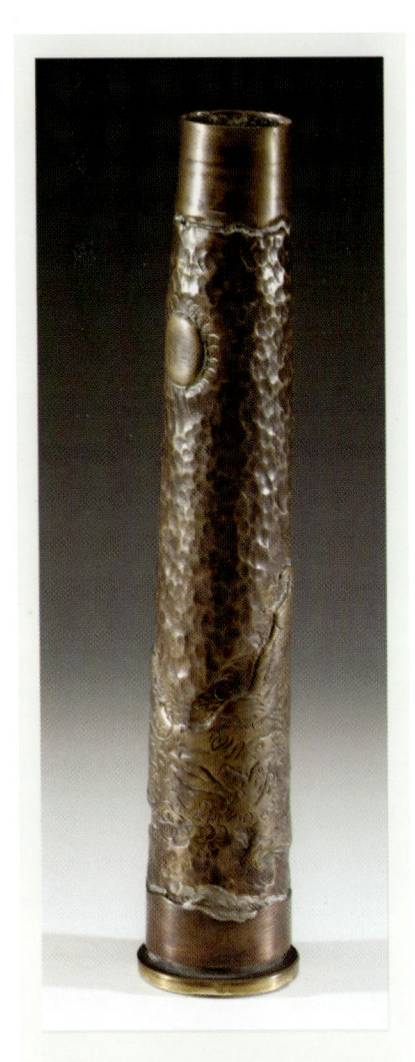

▲ ▶ Trench Art – Finish etched shell casing. Giles O. Lofton Collection of the Institute on WWII, Florida State University.

Giles O. Lofton's basic training was in Bainbridge, Maryland, and he was later assigned to the USS Wisconsin, a battleship of the 3rd Fleet under Admiral William "Bull" Halsey. The ship engaged in combat at Leyte, Lingayen Gulf, Iwo Jima, and Okinawa, taking part in the bombardment of the Japanese Home Islands toward the end of the war. Lofton's two empty artillery shell casings provided an opportunity for Lofton to create what is usually described as "trench art," creative works made by service members using military related materials during lulls in the fighting. Lofton etched the outline of a woman onto one of the casings that he later transformed into the base for a lamp. It has since been returned to its original trench art appearance.

BIBLIOGRAPHIES & FURTHER READINGS

Ambrose, Stephen E. *Citizen Soldiers: The US Army from the Normandy Beaches to the Bulge to the Surrender of Germany.* New York: Simon and Schuster, 1997.

Bird, William L., Jr., and Harry R. Rubenstein. *Design for Victory: World War II Posters on the American Home Front.* New York: Princeton Architectural Press, 1998 (The Smithsonian Institution).

Bodnar, John. *The "Good War" in American Memory.* Baltimore, MD: Johns Hopkins University Press, 2010.

Braddock, Paul F. *Dog Tags: American Military Identification Tag 1861 to 2002.* Chicora, PA: Mechling Publishing, 2003.

Brokaw, Tom. *The Greatest Generation.* New York: Random House, 1998.

Bruscino, Thomas. *A Nation Forged in War: How World War II Taught Americans to Get Along.* Knoxville: University of Tennessee Press, 2010.

DePastino, Todd. *Bill Mauldin: A Life Up Front.* New York: W.W. Norton & Company, 2008.

DePastino, Todd, ed. *Willie and Joe: the WWII Years.* 2 vols. Seattle: Fantagraphics, 2008.

Foster III, LTC Hugh F. "The Infantry Soldier's Load, Winter of 1944-45." 45th Infantry Division. Last modified February 24, 2010. Accessed September 5, 2014. http://www.45thdivision.org/Pictures/General_Knowlege/combatload.htm.

Kennedy, David M. *Freedom from Fear: The American People in Depression and War, 1929-1945.* New York: Oxford University Press, 1999.

Kjeldbaek, Esben, ed. *The Power of the Object: Museums and World War II.* Edinburgh: MuseumsEtc, 2009.

Linderman, Gerald F. *The World Within War: America's Combat Experience in World War II.* New York: Free Press, 1997.

Knightley, Philip. *The First Casualty: From Crimea to Vietnam: The War Correspondent as Hero, Propagandist, and Myth Maker.* New York: Harcourt Brace Jovanovich, 1975.

Mauldin, Bill. *Sicily Sketch Book.* Palermo: IRES, 1943.

Mauldin, Bill. *This Damn Tree Leaks.* Italy: The Stars and Stripes Mediterranean, 1945.

Mauldin, Bill. *Up Front.* New York: H. Holt and Co., 1945.

Mauldin, Bill. *Back Home.* New York: W. Sloan Associates, 1947.

Mauldin, Bill. *A Sort of a Saga.* New York: W. Sloan Associates, 1949.

Mauldin, Bill. *The Brass Ring: A Sort of Memoir.* New York: Norton, 1971.

Meyer, Leisa D. *Creating GI Jane: Sexuality in the Women's Army Corps During World War II.* New York: Columbia University Press, 1998.

Pyle, Ernie and David Nichols. *Ernie's War: The Best of Ernie Pyle's World War II Dispatches.* New York: Random House, 1986.

Overy, Richard. *Why the Allies Won.* New York: Norton, 1995.

Piehler, G. Kurt and Sidney Pash. *The United States and the Second World War: New Perspectives on Diplomacy, War, and the Home Front.* New York: Fordham University Press, 2010.

Roeder, George H., Jr. *The Censored War: American Visual Experience During World War II.* New Haven, CT: Yale University Press, 1993.

Rowe, Patrick M., ed. *Bill Mauldin: A Selection of Paintings, Drawings, and Prints from the Rowe Collection.* Pensacola: University of West Florida, The Art Gallery, 2012.

Sharnick, John and Oliver Gregg Howard. *Stripes: The First Five Years of the GI's Newspaper.* Pfungstadt, 1947.

Smith, Jill Halcomb. *Dressed for Duty: America's Women in Uniform, 1898-1973.* San Jose, CA: R. James Bender, 2003.

Stanton, Capt. Shelby L. *US Army Uniforms of World War II.* Mechanicsburg, PA: Stackpole Books, 1994. http://www.history.army.mil/html/bookshelves/collect/ww2-ts.html.

Takaki, Ronald T. *Double Victory: A Multicultural History of America in World War II.* Boston, MA: Little, Brown, 2000.

Windrow, Richard. *The World War II GI: US Army Uniforms 1941-45 in Colour Photographs.* Wiltshire, UK: The Crowood Press UK, 2008.

Wouters, Marcel. "Objects and the Power of their Stories." In *The Power of the Object: Museums and World War II,* edited by Esben Kjeldbæk, 2. Edinburgh: MuseumsEtc, 2009. Accessed June 26, 2014. http://www.woutersontwerpers.nl/wp-content/uploads/2009/07/The-Power-of-the-Object-EN-DE.pdf.

Zuljan, Ralph. "Allied and Axis GDP." *Articles On War 4* (July 1, 2003): 1. Accessed September 5, 2014. http://www.onwar.com/articles/0302.htm#.

WORLD WAR II WRITERS' WEEKEND
Selected books by Authors of the Writers' Weekend

Bendeck, Whitney. *"A" Force: The Origins of British Deception During the Second World War.* Annapolis, MD: Naval Institute Press, 2013.

Cox, Marcus. *Segregated Soldiers: Military Training at Historically Black Colleges in the Jim Crow South.* Baton Rogue: Louisiana State University Press, 2013.

Culver, Annika. *Glorify the Empire: Japanese Avant-Garde Propaganda in Manchukuo.* Vancouver, BC: University of British Columbia Press, 2014.

Dunbar, Peter. *Before They Were the Black Sheep.* Gainesville, FL: University Press of Florida, 2011.

Gellately, Robert. *Stalin's Curse: Battling for Communism in War and Cold War.* New York: Vintage, 2013.

Kohnstam, Pieter. *A Chance to Live: A Family's Journey to Freedom.* Sarasota, FL: Bardolf & Co., 2006.

McCall, Jack H., Jr. *Pogiebait's War: A Son's Quest for His Father's Wartime Life.* Xlibris, 2001.

Neiberg, Michael. *The Blood of Free Men: The Liberation of Paris.* New York: Basic Books, 2012.

FLORIDA STATE UNIVERSITY

John E. Thrasher, President • Garnett S. Stokes, Provost and Executive Vice President for Academic Affairs • Peter Weishar, Dean, College of Fine Arts • Sam Huckaba, Dean, College of Arts & Sciences

INSTITUTE ON WORLD WAR II AND THE HUMAN EXPERIENCE, DEPARTMENT OF HISTORY, COLLEGE OF ARTS AND SCIENCES

William Oldson (1940-2014), Founding Director

G. Kurt Piehler, Director • Anne Marsh, Administrative Assistant • Hillary Sebeny, Graduate Assistant • Richard Siegler, Graduate Assistant (Summer 2014) • Jordan Bolan, Undergraduate Assistant • Luke Cochran, Intern (Summer 2014) • Jennifer Barton, Volunteer • Sheri Davis, Volunteer • Richard Davis, Volunteer • Chris Juergens, Volunteer • Mary LePoer, Volunteer • Elizabeth McLendon, Volunteer • Inez Manuel, Volunteer • Sharyn Heiland Shields, Volunteer • Shannon Thomas, Volunteer • Dorothy Whittle, Volunteer • Joan Denman, Archivist Emeritus • Rachel Stuart Duke, Graduate Assistant / Volunteer

MUSEUM ADVISORY COMMITTEE

Jessica Comas, CFA Senior Development Officer • Jack Freiberg, CFA Associate Dean • David Gussak, Chair, Art Education • Carolyn Henne, CFA Associate Dean & Chair, Art Department • Lynn Hogan, CFA Associate Dean • Cameron Jackson, Director, School of Theatre • Adam Jolles, Chair, Art History • Allys Palladino-Craig, Director, Museum of Fine Arts • Patty Phillips & Russell Sandifer, Co-Chairs, School of Dance • Lisa Waxman, Chair, Interior Design

MUSEUM OF FINE ARTS STAFF

Allys Palladino-Craig, Director & Editor-in-Chief, MoFA Press • Jean D. Young, Registrar & Publications Designer • Teri R. Abstein, Curator of Education & Graduate Museum Studies • Wayne T. Vonada, Jr., Preparator & Installations Designer • Rosalina Zindler, Fiscal Officer & Departmental Representative • Jasmine Van Weelden, Communications & Membership Coordinator • Rebecca Ryan, Events Staff • Tom Wylder, Events Staff

MUSEUM INTERNS AND VOLUNTEERS

Maize Arendsee, Teaching Assistant • Danielle Awad, Volunteer • Annie L. Booth, Volunteer Coordinator • Colleen Bowen, Research Assistant • Sarah E. Cass, Intern • Christina Cha, Volunteer • Brandi Frazier, Intern • Azure Green, Intern • Krista T. Keitzman, Intern • Megan Moran, Volunteer • Shannon I. Nortz, Volunteer • Ashley N. Wallace, Volunteer • Veronica Zingarelli, Research Assistant